MORRIS ON
TYING FLIES

Skip Morris

Frank
Amato
PORTLAND

Carol Ann Morris

Carol Ann Morris

Published in 2006 by
Frank Amato Publications, Inc.
PO Box 82112 • Portland, Oregon 97282 • (503) 653-8108 • www.amatobooks.com
Softbound ISBN: 1-57188-378-9 • Softbound UPC: 0-81127-00212-2

All photographs taken by Skip Morris unless otherwise noted
Front Cover Photo: Carol Ann Morris
Front Cover Photo Insets: Top to bottom, Skip Morris, Carol Ann Morris, Skip Morris, Skip Morris
Back Cover Photos: Carol Ann Morris
Cover Design: Tony Amato
Book Design: Leslie Brannan
Printed in Singapore

1 3 5 7 9 10 8 6 4 2

TABLE OF CONTENTS

DRY FLIES 6

The King's River Caddis	7	The Bi-Visible	18
The Midge	8	The Fluttering Salmon Fly (or the F150)	19
The Madam X	9	The Royal Coachman and Coachman Trudes	21
The Gulper Special	11	The Tom Thumb	23
The Ant Carol	13	The Chernobyl Ant	25
Standard Variations on Standard Dry Flies	15		

NYMPHS 27

The Feather Duster	28	The Royal Flush	34
The Zebra Midge	29	The Montana Stone	37
Bird's Stonefly Nymph	30	Egg Flies	38
The Halfback	32	The Green Damsel	42
The Gray Nymph	33	Scud Flies	44

EMERGERS, SOFT HACKLES, AND A WET FLY 47

The Foam PMD Emerger	48	Soft-Hackled Flies	50
The Dark Cahill Wet Fly	49	The Partidge Caddis Emerger	53

GROUPED DRY FLIES, NYMPHS, EMERGERS, AND SUCH 54

Tying Tiny for Fall Trout	55	Three Flies for the Great Western Caddis	63
Kamloops Stillwater Standards	58		

STREAMERS AND BUCKTAILS 68

The Peacock Chenille Leech	69	The Lefty's Deceiver	77
The Half and Half	70	The Zonker in General, and a Variation in Particular	79
Streamers and Bucktails for Spring Streams	73		

BASS AND PAN FISH FLIES 82

Tap's Bug	83	The McGinty	87
The Silver Outcast	85		

FLIES FOR ATLANTIC SALMON, STEELHEAD, PACIFIC SALMON, AND MIGRATORY TROUT 89

The Bomber and the Green Machine	90	Light and Dark Flies for Summer Steelhead	102
Three New Flies for Sea-Runs	94	The Egg-Sucking Leech	107
The Raccoon	98		

THE ARTICLES IN MORRIS ON TYING FLIES 110

INDEX 111-112

ACKNOWLEDGMENTS

I asked for and received lots of help with *Morris on Tying Flies*. Thus I offer my thanks to all those whose contributions make this book as good as I—or rather we—could make it.

FOR THEIR HELP WITH THE ORIGINAL ARTICLES

Thanks to my old friend Rick Hafele, the entomologist, for helping me figure out the details of so many of the aquatic insects that some of the flies imitate; to Lefty Kreh for helping me with his Lefty's Deceiver and his and Bob Clouser's Half and Half (and for kick-starting my entire career in fly fishing); to Dave Hughes for all that information on fishing and entomology, and for two decades of friendship; to Brian Chan for his unfailing willingness to share his fly patterns, insights, or both; to guide Mike Seim for testing my own fly designs on his wonderful Yellowstone-area rivers; to Dave Pond for those grand float trips down the Deschutes River and his help in drifting the Brick Back Caddis through miles of trout water; to Al Troth for sharing the details of his many excellent fly patterns over the years; to Peter Morrison for all the fine fishing he's provided Carol and me on his home rivers, for helping me test all sorts of fly patterns there, and simply for his companionship; to Art Scheck for all his ideas about fly patterns, especially his monumental words regarding the imitative properties of the McGinty wet fly; to Jim Kerr for his sage advice regarding egg and sea-run cutthroat flies; to Ken Mitchell for a grand fly-testing adventure in Alaska; to Troy Dettman for introducing me to the John Day River and for his advice on flies for summer steelhead; to Jeffery Delia for all the opportunities he's provided me to refine my fly patterns on his estuary cutthroats; to Bill Demchuck for some great fishing trips and opportunities for fly-testing; to Todd Smith for helping me figure out his Fluttering Salmon Fly and for showing me and Carol some hot—both literally and figuratively—fishing out of Boise, Idaho; to Shawn Bennett for those magnificent salmon and pugnacious rockfish out of Tofino, British Columbia, Canada; to Mike Harves for introducing me to the Madam X (and the *real* Yakima River); to Ken Fujii for help with his deadly Zebra Midge; to Mike Lawson for details on his Partridge Caddis Emerger; to Gordon Honey for details of, and his seasoned perspective on, Canadian lake flies; to Bob Jacklyn, winner of the Federation of Fly Fishers' Buz Buszek tying award, for information on and a sample of his Jacklin's Giant Salmon Fly; to Rod Bringle for help with his Rod's Sculpin; to guide Tom Baltz for a grand tour of the legendary Letort and posing for the camera with all those minscule flies.

FOR THEIR HELP WITH THE BOOK

First, my thanks to Carol Ann Morris, my wonderful wife of eleven years, the veterinarian who surprised everyone—herself, perhaps, most of all—by tackling the camera and paintbrush as she'd tackle a difficult surgery and then producing richer and richer images; she shot many of the photos and painted all the illustrations in this book. Thanks to Tony Amato and Leslie Brannan for their tasteful layout; to Ted Leeson for chasing down questionable commas, dangling constructions, and such; and to Frank Amato, whose considered perspective made *Morris on Tying Flies* better than it would have otherwise been.

TO THE EDITORS

It was the editors who really catalyzed *Morris on Tying Flies*. They did so by telling me to go ahead with so many of my magazine proposals, and thus turned mere intentions into the actual articles that make up this book. Over the years, many editors have come and gone—too many for me to thank here individually. So I offer my broad but sincere thanks to you all.

INTRODUCTION

Within these pages are most of my favorite fly-tying pieces to date. That's saying something, since I figure I've written around two hundred articles for the fly-fishing magazines over the past eighteen years or so. Decades-old standards, new hot fly patterns from celebrity tiers, a whole lot between—they're all here. There are seventy-four patterns in this book, including dry flies; nymphs; streamers and bucktails; emergers; steelhead and Atlantic salmon flies; flies for bass (both largemouth and smallmouth) and pan fish; flies for tropical saltwater fishing and even some flies for salt waters North. Quite a range, eh?

I started this project with pure intentions: to preserve (as much as possible) the original content of these articles. I mean *original* content, just as they looked when my printer first spat them out, before the magazines began kneading and carving them. Oh sure, I allowed myself an adjustment here and there, a yanked comma, an extra photo slipped into a blank space or one in a series reshot—but only when absolutely necessary. I sorted through all the nouns and verbs, colons and commas and dashes, following carefully my noble directive of noninterference. When the deed was all done, I sat smiling at the manuscript on my desk and bathing in the glow of accomplishment, but gradually realized the glow was suffering a brownout, and paused in a frown... Then I said, "To hell with it" and rewrote like a madman. I shot a bunch of new photos, too, and put my photographer-wife on assignment. I also served notice on her watercolor skills, and got a pile of new paintings for the book.

The plain truth is, I couldn't resist. I couldn't let those articles, some written more than a decade ago, stand absent information I'd since learned and with prose I could better craft. Now, with my radical renovation completed and the results before me, I feel satisfied that I made the right choice. And that formerly dim glow of accomplishment is up to full wattage.

In the end, we all win—I'm satisfied that I've done my best, you get a better book, and Frank Amato, my publisher, can add this title to his list with pride.

To hell with lofty but misguided intentions about "original content."

So that's the story—why these particular articles are here and why they may seem different (*better*, I hope) than when you might have first seen them in five different magazines. Enough said. I shouldn't and won't take any more of your time on the matter. Better you spend it with the pages that follow.

Happy tying!

Skip Morris

Dry Flies

A wild cutthroat taken on a small dry fly and released.

The famous salmonfly stonefly.

Silver Creek in Idaho is a rich spring creek where tiny dry flies are common and trout are magnificently obstinate.

All photos by Carol Ann Morris

THE KING'S RIVER CADDIS

HOOK: Light wire, standard length to 1X long, sizes 16 to 10.

THREAD: Brown 8/0 or 6/0.

BODY: Raccoon fur or natural or synthetic brown dubbing.

WING: Mottled-brown turkey primary.

HACKLE: Brown.

Named for the California river of its birth, the King's River Caddis is among those flies you want to tie just because it looks so good. Its clean lines and crisply notched wing of cinnamon-and-cream radiate elegance.

It is this distinctive wing that set the King's River Caddis, an otherwise conventional fly, apart from other adult-caddis imitations during the height of its popularity in the 1950s and 60s. (It is, admittedly, a somewhat fragile wing, but a coating of flexible cement can improve that.)

Despite concerns that it's too pretty to be good, too fragile to be useful, the King's River Caddis continues catching trout, just as it has for decades.

Wayne "Buz" Buszek of Visalia, California, for whom the "Buz Buszek" fly-tying award was named, created the King's River Caddis.

1. Start the thread on the hook's shank, and then dub a full body over the rear two thirds of the shank.

2. Snip a section about as wide as the hook's gape from a mottled-brown turkey primary. Trim a notch in the tip of the section. (A light coating of Dave's Flexament increases durability.)

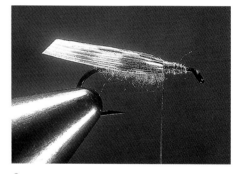

3. Bind the section, by its un-notched butt, atop the front of the dubbed body. The notched end of the section should extend past the end of the body a distance about equal to the hook's gape. Trim off the butt of the section.

4. Strip the soft fibers from the bases of two dry-fly hackles appropriate to the hook's size. Bind the hackles at the front of the wing. Trim the hackles' stems and bind their cut ends. End with the thread hanging just behind the hook's eye.

5. Wind one hackle forward in slightly open spirals; then bind its tip. Wind the second hackle forward through the first; then bind its tip. Trim both tips and then build and complete a thread-head. Coat the head with head cement to complete the King's River Caddis.

A real caddisfly adult—notice any resemblance to the King's River Caddis?

THE MIDGE

HOOK: Standard dry fly (or short shank), sizes 18 to 26.

THREAD: Eight-ought (or even finer), normally in a color to match the body.

TAIL: Hackle fibers, in a color to match the body.

BODY: Dubbing or thread in most any reasonable fly color. Most common are cream, blue dun, black, brown, and olive.

HACKLE: One, in a color to match the body.

The term "midge" gets tossed around by fly fishers in ways often foggy, and sometimes plain confusing. Its several separate meanings aren't always easy to distinguish. They are (1) *any* tiny insect upon which trout feed (2) a specific insect (usually tiny) called a chironomid (3) any fly that imitates a chironomid (4) any fly that imitates *any* tiny insect (5) any one in a series of dry-fly dressings that imitates tiny insects upon which trout feed; the "M" is lowercase for this midge series in general, but capitalized for specific patterns.

So if you hear the word "midge," listen carefully for the specific meaning the speaker has in mind.

In the midge series of fly patterns (meaning #5) each variation adds a preceding word to identify its particular mix of materials or colors or both. The *Black* Midge, for example, is entirely black; the *Adams* Midge bears the grizzly and brown hackles of the original Adams and is the only well-known, two-hackle midge. Other patterns in the series abound.

But a fly in the midge series will have characteristics other than just the word "Midge" in its name, specifically, a tiny hook, an absence of the usual dry-fly wings (though a few variations have them), and a simple tail-body-hackle form.

Most anglers use the midge series of flies to imitate tiny chironomids and mayflies. Any time you are trout fishing may be a good time for a midge, but winter is especially good. Winter, you see, is when most insects are quiet, so the two insects that most commonly hatch in the cold months become especially attractive to trout. Those two insects are the chironomid (again, also known as the midge) and the mayfly *Baetis*. Both are tiny, and both are fine subjects for imitating with midges—midges, that is, with a capital "M."

1. Start the thread about three quarters up the hook's shank. Strip off some fibers from a hackle and bind them along the top the shank to the hook's bend. The resulting tail should about equal the entire length of the hook.

2. Trim closely the butts of the hackle fibers. Dub a slender body up three quarters of the shank. Use very little dubbing, either natural or synthetic. (I prefer synthetic dubbing in dry flies—it doesn't absorb water.)

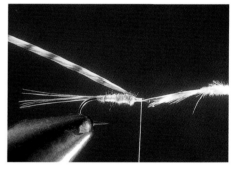

3. Strip the long, soft fibers from the base of a hackle. Bind the hackle by its bare stem to the front of the body. Trim the hackle's stem closely. End with the thread hanging just behind the hook's eye.

4. Wind the hackle forward in three or four close turns. (Tiny flies don't require much hackle.) Bind the hackle at the eye, trim away the hackle's tip, whip finish the thread, trim it, and coat the whip finish with head cement.

5. Many tiers prefer to form the body of a midge from bare working thread, like the Cream Midge shown here. So little dubbing is used in a midge, to keep the body slender, that they just eliminate it altogether.

Carol Ann Morris

A real midge, specifically, an adult chironomid.

THE MADAM X

HOOK:	Light wire, 2X or 3X long, sizes 8 and 6.
THREAD:	Yellow 3/0.
BODY and TAIL:	Natural deer hair (or elk).
WING and HEAD:	Natural deer hair (but I prefer elk hair, because it makes a tougher head).
LEGS:	Round white rubber-strand.

Not long after the Madam X made its debut in Doug Swisher's videotape, "Tying Attractor Flies," I happened to be standing in a trout stream with a friend who began raving about the deadliness of this peculiar new dry fly. "The fly shop's out of it again," he said, as if to validate his account. Still uncertain I was properly impressed, he added, "They just can't keep it in stock!"

Few flies burst onto the scene with such bravado. I *was* impressed...but, it seemed, so was everyone else. Everyone still seems impressed with the Madam X.

Variations: on the left, a Madam X with an all-floss body (and the yellow legs Skip often substitutes for the standard white); on the right, an orange version with a saddle hackle palmered up the body.

Carol Ann Morris

Undercut banks—a fine place to put a Madam X. But I've seen good trout come right up from the bottom in the middle of a deep pool for this fly, so feel free to try it anywhere.

Just who created the Madam X I'm not sure. Doug Swisher probably developed the fly, and is usually given credit for it, but in his video he never plainly says so.

He does say that he was "almost afraid" to tell anyone about the Madam X for quite a while. It is an alarming trout fly, with its crisscrossed ribs, thick tail, and gangly cross of legs. He finally did tell because the Madam X kept catching trout. Doug says that he usually fishes it along stream banks and back under overhanging grasses and cut banks. He fishes it either dead drift or with twitches. When a trout takes a Madam X, he says, the result is "usually explosive." Its long springy legs may be what

sets the Madam X apart from other attractor dry flies; Doug says that because of those legs, the fly "vibrates."

There is nothing particularly delicate or graceful about the Madam X; it has more the coarse bulk of a bass bug than the intricate lightness of most trout flies. Doug completely eradicates any possible resemblance to a normal dry fly by tying it on really big hooks. He explains his choice of hook on the videotape: "Fish like a big bite, not a small bite," he says.

Most popular fly patterns spawn a seemingly endless procession of variations—who hasn't seen a dozen versions of the Woolly Bugger? In general, this is a form of flattery; without question, it signals a fly's popularity. Some of the fly-pattern books in my collection describe Madam Xs with bodies of a solid layer of thread or floss over the deer hair, instead of the original spiraled thread-crosses up a deer-hair body. Others list orange thread as an option to replace the standard yellow. I've even seen a pattern with a brown hackle palmered up the body. My own touch is to use *yellow* rubber-strand legs in place of the standard white.

I'll show you how to tie the Madam X as I tie it, my personal style, though this fly's form largely dictates the method of its tying.

1. Start the thread at the hook's bend; then wind it tightly up two thirds of the hook's shank. Comb and stack a small bunch of deer (or elk) hair. Bind the hair by its butts at the two-thirds-up-the-shank point. The hairs' tips should extend beyond the rear of the shank a distance roughly equal to the hook's gape.

2. Trim the butts closely. Hold the hair down around the shank as you wind the thread down the hair in tight open spirals to the bend. At the bend, add two turns; then spiral the thread back up to the front of the hair. Take a few tight thread-turns at the front of the body to lock the spiraled turns in place. The hair-body should now have a pattern of thread-Xs along it.

3. Comb and stack another small bunch of deer (I use elk) for the head and wing. Hold the hair so that its tips are even with the tips of the tail; then cut the hair's butts straight across about 1/4 inch beyond the hook's eye.

4. Bind the hair, by its butts, from the eye back to the front of the body. The tips of the hair should point forward, over the hook's eye. Try to keep the hair entirely atop the hook's shank as you bind it on.

5. With the thread hanging at the front of the body, stroke the wing-hair up, and then pull it back and down. Bind the hair in place with a few tight thread-turns. You now have a wing and a sort of half bullet-head, both atop the hook. Ideally, the wing's tips should be even with the tail's tips.

6. Bind a short length of rubber-strand along each side of the thread collar with tight thread-turns at the rear of the head. Draw back the legs and whip finish the thread just in front of them. (Doug prefers to whip finish the thread at the hook's eye, in front of the bullet head.) Trim the thread.

7 Trim the legs long—for example, when the rear legs are pressed back against the sides of the fly, they should reach to the tips of the tail, or even slightly beyond. Add head cement to the whip finish.

THE GULPER SPECIAL

HOOK:	Light wire, standard length to 1X long (standard dry-fly hook), sizes 22 to 12 (size 18 to 24 for *Tricorythodes*).
THREAD:	Eight-ought or 6/0 in a color to blend with the body (brown 8/0 for *Tricorythodes*).
WING:	Poly yarn in white, orange, yellow, or green (or whatever color you can best see).
HACKLE:	Any reasonable mayfly color (grizzly for *Tricorythodes*).
TAIL:	Hackle fibers, same color as the hackle.
BODY:	Synthetic dubbing (dark-brown for *Tricorythodes*).

The simple and logical, bright, and durable Gulper Special is a solid imitation of a mayfly adult. Or to be more accurate, a *near-adult*—it's what fly fishers call a "dun," a mayfly transformed from an underwater creature to a flying creature of the air, yet not fully matured for mating. In various sizes and colors the Gulper Special can suggest duns of many species, but I think of one mayfly in particular when I think of this fly.

That mayfly is the diminutive late-summer- and fall-hatching *Tricorythodes* (long name for a short bug). When it emerges from lazy currents in streams or the still water of lakes in its characteristic abundance, trout often move to the easy feast it presents.

Those trout have plenty of living samples of *Tricorythodes* to compare against the angler's flies, and in such quiet water have plenty of time to inspect what they eat, or refuse. It's a real challenge for the angler—getting the fly to drift right up to a fish, keeping that drift natural and free, and striking and playing fish on the requisite gossamer tippets. Of course none of that matters unless the fly on that tippet is true of size, color, posture, and form.

The Gulper Special, tied very small in black or dark-brown, is just such a fly—a match for a "Trico," the nickname for *Tricorythodes*—and is the standard *Tricorythodes* imitation for many keen fly fishers.

Al Troth, who gave us the Troth Pheasant Tail and the ubiquitous Elk Hair Caddis, created the Gulper Special.

From late summer into fall across North America , the surface of spring creeks—or any cold-water lazy, silty stream, even lakes—will grow matted each morning with masses of hatching Tricorythodes *duns.*

A Tricorythodes *dun. The male is dark-brown overall, with three long tails. This is the female. Her abdomen is olive, her thorax dark-brown. Her tails are shorter than those of the male.*

Carol Ann Morris

1. Bind a short length of poly yarn (any color that will be easy to see) crossways atop the hook's shank, about three quarters up the shank. Grasp the ends of the yarn and pull firmly, forcing the yarn to the underside of the shank.

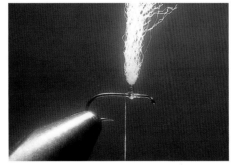

2. Draw up the ends of the yarn and bind them together tightly. Wrap a layer of thread lightly up and down the yarn's base.

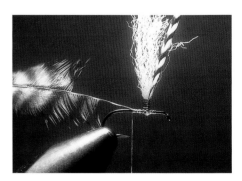

3. Bind a hackle by its stripped stem up, then back down the bindings at the base of the yarn (you can wrap the thread more tightly than before); then bind the stem back along the shank a little ways. Trim the hackle's stem.

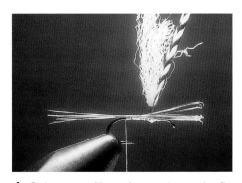  

4. Strip some fibers from a large dry-fly hackle and bind them along the shank as a tail. Trim the butts of the fibers, near the yarn-wing. The tails should extend from the hook's bend about one full hook's length. (Though for *Tricorythodes* specifically, you could make the tails longer.)

5. Dub a tapered body from the hook's bend forward to just back from its eye. Make sure you cover everything around the base of the wing with dubbing—this is an easy spot to leave unfinished, with thread showing through gaps.

6. Wind the hackle down the thread-layered base of the poly yarn to the body. Draw back the hackles from the hook's eye and bind the tip of the hackle to the shank, just back from the eye. Trim the hackle-tip away, then complete the usual thread head. Coat that head with head cement.

Trim the wing to a point, just slightly shorter than the hook's full length.

(For more on creating a parachute hackle, see "Standard Variations on Standard Dry Flies.")

Spider web with Tricos.

THE ANT CAROL

HOOK:	Light wire, standard length to 1X long (standard dry-fly hook), sizes 12 and 10 (smaller or larger for imitating flying ants other than the termite, size 20—even smaller if you dare—up to size 8, though I seldom go smaller than 14 and never larger than 8).
THREAD:	Red 8/0 or 6/0 (for versions other than the red-orange termite, thread-color should echo body-color).
ABDOMEN:	Red-orange synthetic dubbing (or some other ant-color, typically black or brown) poly, Superfine, Antron...
WINGS:	Brown buck tail.
THORAX:	The same as the abdomen.
HACKLE:	One, brown (or whatever color imitates the natural).

Flying ants, though the fishing books and magazines seldom mention them, can be serious business to the fly fisher. I've seen flying ants as tiny as size-24 hooks sprinkled like gray dust over the surface of a Montana lake; and I've caught good trout out in water sixty feet deep that were hunting the surface for flying ants with thick brown bodies. But where I live—on Washington State's Olympic Peninsula—the most important flying ant is the termite. Brown-orange bodied with long brown wings, it begins its nervous flights in the hot evenings of mid-August and continues them into the first part of September. It's big, as trout-food insects go, calling for a size-10 or -12 hook for imitation, and it can hit the lakes in respectable numbers on the best days. I've seen largemouth bass uncharacteristically far out from shore quietly picking termites from the surface like trout. And I'm sure that bluegills and some of the other pan fishes also occasionally focus on termites. But despite that other fishes have a taste for them, termites and all other flying ants I think of as trout food. And though termites and their relatives must drop onto streams, again becoming fare for trout, I nonetheless think of them as trout food of lakes.

My imitation of the termite, the Ant Carol, evolved over two decades of hunting lakes for trout (and sometimes bass) that were themselves hunting termites. It sort of developed on its own, along that oft-mentioned path of least resistance, replacing or revising inefficient aspects of its design and shedding unnecessary parts along the way. Simplicity in a fly pattern (that is, a fly pattern intended for fish rather than for displaying behind glass) must always be a virtue, and the Ant Carol is simple indeed. It's bucktail wings are spare enough to suggest the veined translucent-brown wings of the natural, supple enough to flex and let the hook do its job, stiff enough to hold their shape through the rigors of riding out casts and catching fish. Its body of synthetic dubbing is buoyant (like the wings, when they've been treated with floatant). Its hackle is sparse enough to suggest a few legs. One could start over with a whole new design to improve buoyancy—extend the body and reduce the mass of the hook; make the body of something incapable of absorbing water, like closed-cell foam—but that would make a heavier demand on the tier, and there is no pressing need for great buoyancy in a dry fly that, like the Ant Carol, is only quietly manipulated on standing water. Besides, flying ants seem heavy and their fall to water is usually harsh, so they often wind up a bit low in the surface of the water...about as low in the surface as an Ant Carol lies.

A simple fly for a simple job. But an effective fly, especially when fish are seeking flying ants atop lakes.

A termite.

Carol Ann Morris

Various colors and sizes.

1. Start the thread at the hook's bend. Dub a full, rounded abdomen over the rear third of the hook's shank. (You can dub down the bend a little, if you like.)

2. Cut a small bunch of hair from the natural-brown area of an undyed buck tail. Use the long stiff hairs, not the short soft ones. Comb out the short hairs and under-fur. Stack the hairs in a hair-stacking tool. Bind half the hairs on one side of the abdomen, half on the other. The abdomen should push the two bunches out to the sides in a shallow "V". The length of the wings should equal the full length of the hook, or be *slightly* longer.

3. Bind the butts of the hairs tightly along the shank to just back from the hook's eye. Trim the butts. Build another bulge of dubbing just behind the eye. Build it to only about half to two-thirds the length and diameter of the abdomen. End with the thread *behind* the dubbing.

(An alternate approach for the wings: bind them as a single bunch atop the hook, right back to the abdomen, then split them with crisscrossed turns of thread.)

4. Spiral the thread back to the wings and take a turn or two of thread around each, if needed, to gather them into distinct bunches. Remember that *tight* thread-turns will flare the hair, *firm* turns will gather it.

Select a proper-size hackle from a dry-fly neck or saddle using a hackle gauge. Strip the long, soft fibers from the base of the hackle's stem. Bind the hackle to the shank at the front of the abdomen. Bind the stem along the shank most of the way to the dubbed thorax. Trim the stem closely.

5. Wind the hackle forward in a few open spirals; the result should be sparse. Bind the hackle's tip just short of the thorax. Whip finish the thread behind the thorax, cut it, and add head cement to the whip finish.

You can trim the hackle fibers away underneath, for perhaps a touch more realism, but I haven't yet felt the need.

BLUE DUN *(traditional style)*

HOOK: Light wire, standard length to 1X long (standard dry-fly hook), sizes 18 to 10.

THREAD: Gray 6/0 or 8/0.

WINGS: Mallard-quill sections.

TAIL: Blue-dun hackle fibers.

BODY: Muskrat fur or medium-gray synthetic dubbing.

HACKLE: Blue dun (a bluish medium-gray).

The Adams, the Cahills, the Pale Evening Dun: these dry-fly patterns, like many others of traditional form, are so close in construction that if you can tie one, you are well on your way to tying them all.

And plenty of tiers just leave it at that. When they tie an Adams, for example, they tie it with paired wings, bunched tail, dense hackle collar—the standard configuration—and haven't a thought of tying it any other way. But there are other ways to tie standard dry flies, good ways, worth knowing.

Left to right: the Blue Dun in traditional style, thorax style, and parachute style.

In traditional dry-fly style there is a tail of bunched hackle fibers, a body made from a quill or of dubbing, wings of hackle tips or wood-duck flank or gray duck-primaries, and a collar formed of two dry-fly hackles. The newer thorax-dun and parachute styles are similar to this overall, but alter the wings and hackle, and sometimes the tail.

But why even consider the new styles when traditional dry flies still catch plenty of trout?—because the new dry-fly styles are better...if you believe their supporting arguments. Here are the best such arguments I've heard. The hackle fibers beneath the traditional dry fly may diminish its chances of turning upright before landing on the water, and may even interfere with the hook point's penetration. The thorax and parachute flies have no fibers below; all is on top, clear of the point and above the center of gravity for a sure bite and an upright landing. And then there's posture—mayflies, which traditional dry flies imitate, do not rest on legs and tails, but traditional dry flies do. (Thoraxes and parachutes rest their bodies flat on the water, which isn't always correct either, but most would argue that it's closer).

Debate over the advantages of parachute, thorax, and traditional dry flies won't soon go away—the trout, by continuing to take all three, won't let it. But so what? Tying traditional and parachute and thorax dry flies is challenging and fun—and that's reason enough to tie them all.

TRADITIONAL STYLE

The finer points of traditional styling of a dry fly (at least as it generally stands today; what fly tiers call "traditional" is often at odds with history) include a straight line from tail tip to edge of hackle collar, touching the hook's bend between. (Why? Because, I guess, it looks right to traditionalists.) The wings emerge from the hackle collar's center, their tips stretching upright to just past the the hackle fibers' tips.

Tying the traditional dry fly is old news. So we'll move through it in just a few photographs and captions, which leaves us lots of room in which to explore the newer thorax and parachute styles.

For easy comparison, we'll use just one fly throughout: the Blue Dun.

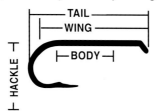

1. Here is a half-finished standard Blue Dun. The tail is hackle fibers; the body is dubbed; the duck-quill-section wings are bound on already, their taper-cut butts covered by the body's dubbing.

  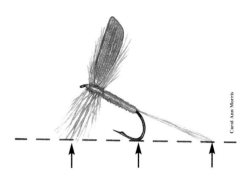

Carol Ann Morris

2. The wings are tugged upright, their bases creased with the thumbnail; then tight thread-turns are built against the wings' base to secure their position. Next, a pair of dry-fly hackles (their bases striped to bare stem) are bound on at the front of the body.

3. The stems of the hackles are trimmed and bound, the thread wound forward nearly to the hook's eye, and then the hackles are wound—one at a time—and secured with thread-turns just behind the eye.

4. The final steps, not shown here, are the trimming of the hackles' tips, the building of a tapered thread head, the whip finishing and trimming of the thread, and the coating of the head with head cement.

Shown above is the classic straight line from tail-tip, touching hook bend, to base of hackle collar.

THORAX STYLE

The original thorax dun was quite different from the versions that followed. Vincent Marinaro, its creator, wasn't too pleased about it, either. Marinaro's fly had precise cut-wings sprouting from a ball of dubbing oddly wrapped with hackle. As you'll soon see, the thorax dun of today lacks these characteristics; nonetheless, most tiers now tie and fish the new version.

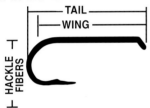

1. Create split tails using any of the standard methods (a few hackle fibers on each side of a ball of thread or dubbing). The tails should be a full hook's length.

Dub a tapered abdomen to about mid-shank.

2. Almost any common dry-fly wings can serve on a thorax dun: paired turkey-flat tips, paired hen-saddle hackles, or a single wing of poly yarn (usually in gray) to name but a few.

Bind the wings (or wing) about three quarters up the hook's shank. Set them upright; divide them, if appropriate. I used the single poly yarn wing here.

3. Strip the base of a single hackle and bind it at mid-shank. Trim the hackle's stem and dub to just behind the eye. Wind the hackle in four to six open turns to the eye. Bind the hackle's tip there, trim it, and then complete a thread head.

4. Trim away the hackle fibers beneath the fly, leaving them flat or in a shallow "V." That completes the Blue Dun Thorax Dun. Though not radically different than the traditional version, it is nonetheless *significantly* different.

PARACHUTE STYLE

Parachute flies are based on the parachute hackle, which they all possess: a horizontal disc of hackle fibers emanating from the base of one wing, all above the weight of the hook's shank—indeed, a sort of parachute to tip the fly upright.

Normally, parachute flies have a single bunched tail, like the traditional dry fly, but an increasing number of new parachute patterns have split tails.

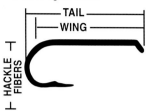

1. The wing of a parachute fly is normally one bunch of white hair or bright poly yarn (orange, yellow, red...).

We'll create a hair wing in this example. Comb and stack a small bunch of white calf-tail hair. Bind the hair atop the hook's shank about three quarters up it. Trim and bind the butts of the hair; then pull the hair firmly back and crease it upright with your thumb nail.

Strip about a dozen long fibers from a big dry-fly hackle and bind them along the shank as a tail.

2. Lock the wing upright by taking a few firm thread-turns around its base, pulling the thread back firmly and then immediately securing it with a few tight turns around the shank.

Wind a layer of the thread a little ways up the base of the wing, then back down—using only *light to modest* thread-tension. The base of the wing will still be pretty flexible through this step.

3. Strip the fluffy and overlong fibers from the base of a hackle that your hackle gauge indicates is of proper size for your hook. Hold the hackle upright, against the base of the wing Wind the thread up the hair and hackle stem and then back down.

The *first* turns stiffened the base of the wing—so you can use *firm* thread-tension this time. Pull the stem of the hackle back along the shank and bind it a little ways. Trim off the end of the stem.

4. Dub the full length of the body, ending with the thread at the hook's eye. Wind the hackle down the base of the wing in close, consecutive turns. Bind the hackle's tip at the eye, whip finish and trim the thread, add head cement to the whip finish.

If you are having trouble working a whip finish past the hackle fibers, try instead slipping a few half hitches over the eye with a half-hitch tool.

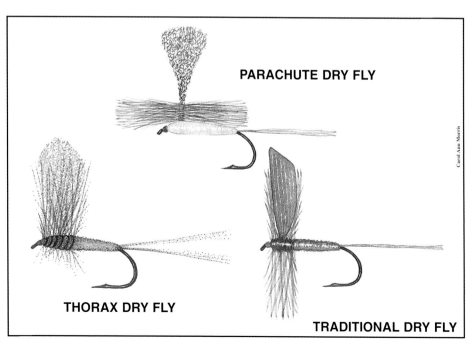

PARACHUTE DRY FLY

THORAX DRY FLY

TRADITIONAL DRY FLY

Carol Ann Morris

THE BI-VISIBLE

HOOK:	Light wire, regular length to 1X long (a standard dry-fly hook), sizes 18 to 10.
THREAD:	Brown 3/0, 6/0, or 8/0.
TAIL:	Brown hackle fibers.
BODY:	Brown hackles, a single white hackle in front.

The Bi-Visible is such a logical dry fly—lots of buoyant hackle with a buoyant tail, capped with a white face like a beacon to the fisherman's eye. During my teenage years, the 1960s, I preferred simple, practical flies for my simple fishing, and the Bi-Visible met my requirements exactly. It was still a popular fly back then, but its popularity seemed to fade as the 70s approached.

But the Bi-Visible is too good a fly to just fade away; many fly fishers still fish it, and still catch fish on it.

At the peak of the Bi-Visible's popularity came the assortment of variations—hackles and tails of black, ginger, blue dun, and grizzly but the standard, at least in my mind, is the brown. When someone says Bi-Visible, I assume they mean a brown one.

It's difficult to say what trout take a Bi-Visible to be—likely some legged, edible thing they've never before seen. But trout probably eat things all the time that they either have never before seen or can't remember having seen; they are, after all, fish—how good can a fish's memory be?

Fortunately, fly fishers' memories are better, good enough, at least, to remember a dependable fly called the Bi-Visible.

1. Start the thread at about the center of the hook's shank. Bind some hackle fibers along the shank as a tail. Bind the butts of the fibers well up the shank. Trim the butts of the fibers (if they are long). The completed tail should be about a full hook's length.

2. Select three appropriate-size hackles from a dry-fly hackle neck (or perhaps just one long dry-fly saddle hackle). Strip the long, soft fibers from the bases of the hackles, leaving only bare stems. Bind the stems from the hook's bend forward to well up the shank.

3. Trim off the hackles' stems just behind the hook's eye. Wind the thread forward to where it hangs about three quarters up the shank. Wind one of the hackles forward in open spirals up three quarters of the shank. Bind the hackle's tip there.

4. Wind another hackle and bind it, as you did the first; then wind the third hackle and bind its tip in the same manner. The idea is to wind the second and third hackles in the slot left between the spirals of the first hackle's stem. Trim the three hackle tips (there are three here, but one is hidden).

5. Prepare a white hackle and bind it by its bare stem at the front of the brown hackles. Trim off the hackle's stem. Advance the thread to slightly short of the eye.

6. Wind the white hackle in close turns to just short of the eye, and then bind the hackle's tip there. Trim away the tip; then build a tapered thread head, whip finish and trim the thread. Add head cement to the head.

THE FLUTTERING SALMON FLY (OR THE F150)

HOOK:	Light to standard wire, 2X or 3X long shank (Todd prefers a curved-shank hook), sizes 6 and 4.
THREAD:	Orange 8/0 or 6/0.
TAIL:	Moose-body hair.
RIB:	Brown saddle hackle.
BODY:	Burnt-orange Antron yarn.
WING:	Elk, sparse, under root beer Krystal Flash, under moose-body hair.
HEAD:	Moose-body hair.
LEGS:	Black rubber-strand.

It happens every spring on the West Coast, every summer in the Rocky Mountain states: new purpose calls the nymph of the legendary salmonfly to creep shoreward from beneath its swift-water stones, climb from the shallows into the air, split and shed its aquatic husk, and rise to its mating once its now-unfurled wings are rigid and dry. Why anglers all but worship this gargantuan stonefly is no mystery: big trout, normally reluctant to rise, will come right up to close their teeth onto a floating salmonfly adult, and will, of course, do the same for an imitation. Big trout on dry flies—trust me, fly fishers will show up for that.

Many famous western rivers sprout salmonflies: Montana's Madison and Big Hole, Wyoming's Green, Oregon's Deschutes, Colorado's Roaring Fork, Alberta, Canada's Bow.

And Idaho's South Fork of the Boise River, which is both why and where Todd Smith—a young production fly tier who spends part of his time behind the counter at the Stonefly Angler fly shop in Boise—developed his Fluttering Salmon Fly (also

The Fluttering Salmon Fly, Todd says, should be fished dead drift near banks, back in the shade under tree limbs and cut-banks on bright days, from afternoon into evening—essentially the standard strategy for fishing any stonefly adult imitation. Halfway through the hatch, however, when spent females fall dying from streamside grasses and tree limbs, Todd takes a different approach. He presses the wing down, flattening and splaying it even further; forgoes floatant; and tries to get the fly sodden, so it will sink or float very low. Then he just tosses it out and lets it drift. The trout see another spent female salmonfly, and...

A Salmonfly adult.

Carol Ann Morris

Bob Jacklin, owner since 1982 of Jacklin's Fly Shop in West Yellowstone, created the Jacklin's Giant Salmon Fly you see above. It is similar enough to Todd Smith's Fluttering Salmon Fly that learning to tie one is learning to tie both. Jacklin's fly, unlike Smith's, has a stub tail (to suggest an egg sack), a rib-hackle of long fibers (trimmed beneath to about halfway between body and hook point), a body of dubbing or Antron yarn, and a wing of blond elk hair set up at a 45-degree angle (to make the fly easy to spot).

known as the F150). It's a predictably huge dry fly, as all salmonfly imitations are, that mimics, specifically, an egg-laying female caught on the water and working her wings to escape. That's why the Fluttering Salmon Fly's wing is splayed. The reason the moose hair in that wing is turned butts-out is to *keep* the wing splayed—Todd found that fine hair-tips, when wet, tend to clump, and destroy the effect. The clean-cut hair-butts in Todd's fly resist clumping *and* create a sharp wing-outline.

TYING TACTICS

A slightly complex but generally straightforward fly at the vise, the Fluttering Salmonfly is nonetheless easier to tie with a few pointers in mind. First, bind the tail butts and the butt of the Antron yarn right up three quarters of the hook's shank—if you cut them short, binding them only at the rear of the shank, you'll wind up building a lumpy-ended body over them. For the rib you'll need a high-quality saddle hackle with short fibers—the kind a hackle gauge would say is right for a size-14 or -16 hook. Bind the hackle by its butt, slightly ahead of the tail—just far enough ahead so that the first turn of yarn settles behind the hackle's stem. The second turn lies in front of the stem. And don't get carried away with the wing—elk hair and moose-body hair together can quickly add up to a mountain of wing. Use enough hair to create a full wing, but no more than that. When you add the Krystal Flash atop the elk hair, bind it on a little forward of the hair, and then stroke it back over and a little down around the hair before you wrap the thread back over its butts—this way the Krystal Flash will spread effectively around the elk, rather than sitting bunched atop it. Try to distribute the butts of the bullet-head hair evenly around the shank so that the resulting head is not overweight on one side and undernourished on the other. Stroke the head-hair back firmly, to even it and create a neat head, but don't pull it back so hard that the hair is strained in the finished head—hair already strained to near its breaking point won't last long against trout teeth.

Enough said. Let's tie.

1. Start the thread at the hook's bend. Cut, comb, and stack in a hair stacker a small bunch of moose-body hair. Bind the hair along the hook's shank as a short tail. Bind a short-fibered saddle hackle by its stripped stem at the bend. Bind Antron yarn along the rear three quarters of the shank to the bend. Spiral the thread back up the shank; then wind the Antron up it in close turns. Bind the end of the Antron and then trim it.

2. Spiral the hackle forward up the body in five or six ribs. Secure the tip of the hackle under tight thread-turns, and then trim off its end.

3. Cut, comb, and stack a small bunch of elk hair. Bind it atop the hook at the front of the body. The wing should reach back to about the tip of the tail. Atop the elk, bind about 20 strands of Krystal Flash. Trim the ends of the Krystal Flash to the same length as the wing. Cut and comb a fair-size bunch of moose-body hair; trim the *butts* of the hair to even, and then bind the hair atop the Krystal Flash—by its *tips*.

Trim closely the forward ends of the Krystal Flash and hair.

4. Cut, comb, and *stack* another substantial bunch of moose-body hair. Bind the hair by its *butts* just behind the hook's eye, hair tips projecting forward a distance about equal to half the shank's length. You want the hair fairly evenly distributed around the shank.

5. With the thread back at the front of the body, draw the hair tips firmly back, and then bind them, creating a bullet head and a short hair-tip collar.

Now, or when the fly is completed, trim the collar-fibers away from the underside, so the fish can see the entire body.

6. Bind a short length of rubber-strand on both sides of the thread-collar behind the bullet head. The result should be two wide-spread legs on the near side and two on the far side of the fly. Whip finish the thread at the center of the legs or directly in front of them. Trim the rear leg-strands to reach back to about the tip of the wing, the forelegs about two thirds this length. Trim the thread, and then add head cement to the whip finish. Fluttering Salmon Fly completed.

THE ROYAL COACHMAN AND LIME COACHMAN TRUDES

ROYAL COACHMAN TRUDE

HOOK: Standard dry fly, sizes 16 to 8.
THREAD: Black 8/0 or 6/0.
TAIL: Golden-pheasant tippets.
BODY: A band of peacock herl at either end of a band of red floss.
WING: White calf tail.
HACKLE: Brown.

LIME COACHMAN TRUDE

Form the body entirely of lime-green dubbing; otherwise, just follow the pattern above for the Royal Coachman Trude.

The Royal Coachman Trude resulted from a sequence of events and ideas as orderly and interconnected as the links of a chain. Over one hundred years ago was born a fanciful upright-wing dry fly called the Royal Coachman. A few decades later, a man named A. S. Trude (or a friend of Trude's, a former mayor of Chicago named Harold Smedly, or both) developed a fly with a horizontal wing of hair. Flies of this style became known as "Trudes." All this happened around the time fly fishers were discovering that trout, despite the old maxim to the contrary, do take dry flies in quick, broken water. The resulting need for dry flies that would stay afloat in the chop sent many anglers to hair-wing flies, but at first, it was flies with *upright* wings, in standard dry-fly form.

The original Royal Coachman dry fly, father of the Royal Coachman Trude and Lime Coachman Trude, is a fly pattern over one hundred years old.

In the meantime, the Royal Coachman was leaving a trail of questionably legitimate offspring in the wake of its soaring popularity—all sorts of new flies called the "Royal" this or "Coachman" that were popping out onto the scene. Eventually the Royal Coachman sired twin sons that sprouted hair wings: the Hair-Wing Royal Coachman and the Royal Wulff. Still on the prowl, the Royal Coachman turned to the sleek, low-winged Trude-type fly and thus was born the Royal Coachman Trude—as predictable an event, considering what lead to it, as any in the world of trout flies (though, at least as I've told it, a bit sordid).

Anyway, that's how I see it after my research: as a chain of thought and events. Others might see it differently—after all, most of this is hearsay. And perhaps they're right. But the old saying tells us that ignorance is bliss, and coincidently I take great delight in my chain-link story.

In any case the Royal Coachman Trude, sometimes known as the Royal Trude (the *Coachman* Trude is yet another and distinct Coachman relative), is a long-time standard dry fly for fast water. It's easy to see because of its white wing, and that wing is easier to create than one that is upright and split.

All the flies of the Royal Coachman family fall under the standard suspicion of any fly that imitates nothing. Why fish the Coachmans instead of flies that suggest mayflies and caddisflies and other foods familiar to trout? Wouldn't something more natural be better? Are the Coachmans really just designed for anglers, and not for their quarry? Such questions as these began with the first non-imitative flies and continue to this day. They shall continue as long as such flies exist.

I can tell you this: I have many times seen trout insist on a particular form of attractor fly and refuse all else. Makes no sense to me but, you know...truth is truth. And that's the truth.

Debates aside, the Royal Coachman Trude has been trusted and fished by many keen anglers over several decades.

Fast, tumbling water—an excellent place to fish a buoyant Trude-style dry fly.

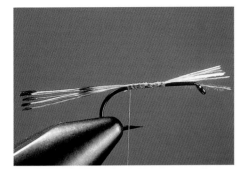

1. Start the thread slightly forward of halfway up the hook's shank. Bind atop the shank a small bunch of tippets, their tips even. Wind the thread down the tippets to the hook's bend. The tippets should project from the bend about a full hook-length.

2. Trim the butts of the tippets closely. Bind a couple of full peacock herls to the shank at the bend. Bind the herls up a bit from their fragile tips. Trim the tips closely.

3. Spin the herls around the thread, to toughen them. Wind the resulting herl-thread rope forward in close turns to create a short band. Secure the herls, at the front of the band, with tight thread-turns.

4. Bind the herls up the shank a bit, and then trim their ends. Bind some red floss to the shank at the front of the herl-band. Advance the thread a little way; then wind the floss forward to create a short floss-band. Secure the end of the floss under tight thread-turns and trim the floss.

5. Create another band of herl, as you did the first. Secure the herls under thread-turns and trim the herls closely. This herl-floss-herl body should cover slightly more than half the shank.

6. Comb and stack a small bunch of calf tail. Bind the bunch atop the hook at the front of the body. The calf should project back to about halfway down the tail. Trim the hair's butts to a taper, and then bind them.

7 Using a hackle gauge, find two neck hackles (or one saddle) appropriate to the size of your hook. Strip the long soft fibers from the base of the stems (or stem). Bind the hackles (or hackle) on at the front of the body and trim the stems. Advance the thread to just behind the hook's eye.

Wind one hackle to the eye in slightly open spirals; then secure it with thread-turns. Wrap the second hackle through the first, and then bind its tip. Trim the stems; build and complete a thread head.

8. The Lime Coachman Trude, another Coachman variation, differs from the Royal Coachman Trude only in the body. To tie the Lime Coachman Trude, simply dub a body of lime-colored fur or synthetic dubbing (I prefer the synthetic dubbing—it's more buoyant than fur), and omit the usual Coachman body of bands of floss and herl.

THE TOM THUMB

HOOK:	Light wire, 1X long (standard dry-fly hook), sizes 14 to 8.
THREAD:	Black 8/0 or 6/0 (or flat waxed nylon or 3/0).
TAIL:	Deer or elk hair.
WING and HUMP:	Deer or elk hair.

In a room full of fly tiers, you could easily pick out some of the Canadians just by looking to see who's tying a Tom Thumb—a lot of Canadians tie the Tom Thumb, and fish it, and likely none of the Americans would ever have even heard of it.

If you looked closer at the work of your Canadians, you'd likely discover that despite an overall similarity, their Tom Thumbs varied. Sometimes, there seem to be as many ways to tie this fly as there are tiers who tie it.

The Tom Thumb has been around for several decades, and I'd guess it to be currently the most popular dry fly in Western Canada, at least for fishing trout lakes. There's a lot more weight in that statement than most Americans would assume, because few of them realize that Western Canada is just chock full of trout lakes—tens of thousands of trout lakes in the province of British Columbia alone, according to Canadian fly-fishing author Brian Chan. Fishing trout lakes is consequently very popular, and serious business, up there.

As good as the Tom Thumb can be on lakes, it *should* be just as effective on streams (though I haven't yet given it enough time on them to say for certain that it is). What it does best is skim or twitch across the surface of water, like a scrambling caddisfly or buzzing back swimmer or even a freshly hatched mayfly dun struggling to work its new wings. The Tom Thumb doesn't look much like any of these insects, really, but as long as it's moving, raking a trail across the surface, it looks like a lot of things through the distortion. And a skimming fly should be just as useful on moving water as on still.

That's the whole thing with the Tom Thumb—making it move. It loves to spread its elongated triangle-wake behind it. If tied correctly, with the wing tipped well forward, it is almost *difficult* to sink. It is the only dry fly I've ever trolled, and one of the very few I'd even consider for such a departure from conventional lake-fishing technique.

The Tom Thumb's history is vague. According to Arthur Lindgren, author of *Fly Patterns of British Columbia*, the Tom Thumb probably came into common use around Jasper, a town in the Canadian province of Alberta, during the 1950s. Lindgren says that a guide named Collie Peacock who ran a fishing-tackle store there "recalled meeting a California dentist who was using the fly in Jasper, but he could not recall the origins of the fly, its name, or that of the dentist fishing it, so he pulled the name 'Tom Thumb' out of his hat." We at least know, then, how the fly got its name. But everything else...murky.

Much clearer, however, is the matter of the Tom Thumb's durability: it's poor. The hump over the back becomes shredded after just a trout of two has had it—even casting can sometimes break a few hairs. But it doesn't seem to matter—trout take it clean or shredded with equal enthusiasm.

I hedge my bet, though. Because I prefer that my Tom Thumbs last as long as possible, I tie them from elk hair, not the usual deer. Elk is much tougher than deer. But even with elk, the fly will look tattered in fairly short order.

I generally use heavy thread for Tom Thumbs, 3/0 and sometimes even flat waxed nylon—thick thread covers the butts of the tail-hair quickly and just makes a tougher fly overall. Of course a lot of tiers intentionally *do not* cover the tail-butts with thread, instead just spiraling the thread over them, in which case the spirals from binding on the tail then mix with the spirals from binding on the wing-hump hair and the whole thing becomes rather uneven and unsightly, though the resulting fly fishes just fine. Try tying it both ways if you like. As I said, there are many ways to tie a Tom Thumb, and trout seem to approve of them all.

The author playing a Kamloops rainbow trout hooked, of course, on a Tom Thumb.

1. Start the thread about three quarters up the hook's shank; then wind it tightly down the shank to the hook's bend. Snip a small bunch of elk hair from the hide, comb out the short hairs and fuzz, and then even the tips in a hair stacker. Measure the hair bunch and then bind it along the shank. The tips should project from the bend a full hook's length.

Prepare a second bunch of hair as you did the first; then hold this second bunch over the first. Even the tips of both.

2. Snip the butts of the second hair-bunch straight across right at the front edge of the hook's eye. Hold the cut edge of the second hair bunch down atop the shank, about halfway up the shank. Bind the hair-butts there, then wind the thread tightly down them to the bend.

3. Cover all the hair along the shank with thread wrappings (that is, if you tie it my way; many would just spiral the thread, letting much of the hair show through). End with the thread hanging about 1/16 of an inch back from the eye. Draw up all the hair from the *second*, top, hair-bunch; pull it forward and down; and then bind it just behind the eye with four to six tight thread-turns. The thread-turns near the eye should be piled, resulting in a narrow collar.

4. Draw the hair-tips firmly back and build tight turns of thread against the front of their base. You want the thread-turns to tip the hairs upright and hold them there securely. But don't overdo it—the fan-wing of hair must tip *forward* a bit. If it is straight upright or tipping back, the fly will dive *under* rather than skim *across* the water.

5. Here's a front view of the wing showing its wide, fanned shape. The photo of the finished fly (on the previous page) shows the wing from the side, gathered flatly. These photos show exactly how the wing *should* look—a flat fan, angled forward, a sort of leaning Comparadun wing.

Complete the Tom Thumb by whip finishing the thread, trimming it, and adding head cement to the whip finish.

THE CHERNOBYL ANT

HOOK:	Light wire, 2X long, sizes 10 to 4.
THREAD:	Orange 3/0.
BODY:	A strip of black closed-cell foam sheeting.
LEGS:	Medium-diameter black round rubber-strand.
INDICATOR:	A strip of yellow closed-cell foam sheeting.

The Chernobyl Ant is a bizarre fly, which, I suppose, is why it's used so often for cutthroat trout—sometimes there's just no making sense of what cutthroats want. However, it's clear to me that they sometimes want a gargantuan ant with crisscrossed legs, which the Chernobyl Ant suggests.

I researched the history of this new fly and most of what little I found came from Jack Dennis's *Tying Flies with Jack Dennis and Friends*. I found that the Chernobyl Ant was created by a guide on Utah's Green River named Allan Woolley, who based his pattern on a fly called the Black Mamba; that Woolley's enormous artificial ant was designed to imitate not an ant at all but a huge western cricket whose numbers explode some years in the grasslands; and that this cricket is called the Mormon cricket, named for its attack on early Mormon crops in Utah.

All well and good, but the Chernobyl Ant, it seems to me, resembles not a cricket but just what its name suggests: an ant, misshapen and absurd in its great bulk—a sort of dark, comic-book mutation resulting from the Russian Chernobyl nuclear tragedy—but an ant nonetheless.

Which brings us back to those cutthroats, whose behavior is often as bizarre as a giant mutant ant. My impression—and that's all it really is—is that the Chernobyl is primarily a cutthroat fly. This impression began during a fishing trip in the fall of 1996.

Mike and Doug had handed my wife Carol and me each a couple of Chernobyl Ants only minutes after we arrived at Yellowstone Park's Slough Creek. "The Creek is full of cutthroats," Mike told us with the quiet confidence of experience, "and cutthroats hardly ever ignore this fly."

"My God," I said, "what's it supposed to be?"

"I really don't know, and I'm sure the cutts don't either. But even if they don't take it, they almost always come up and look it over; then they seem ready to take something else. But a lot of times they just charge up and grab it, even in the middle of a hatch of little mayflies."

"If they'll take this, won't they just take *anything*?"

"Not really. Sometimes it's the *only* thing they'll take."

I looked at the silly gangly-legged monstrosities as though I were looking at a two-headed dog. Mike knows his Yellowstone fishing, and I knew it...but this?

The cutthroats did ignore the Ant that day, but they ignored every other fly we showed them, too. And we showed them plenty—nymphs, streamers, dry flies, big flies, tiny flies, and flies of all sizes in between. Four of us fished for hours and, though we saw a few fish, caught nothing.

Two years later, my friend Peter Morrison called from his home near Cranbrook, in the Southeastern corner of British Columbia, Canada. He and his friend Bill Demchuck were planning a brief break from their guiding operation, Osprey Fly

Slough Creek in Yellowstone National Park, where no fly worked for the author and his wife and friends.

One of the cutthroat rivers in British Columbia, Canada, where the Chernobyl Ant couldn't miss.

Fishing Adventures, to do some...yes, some fishing, of course.

"Brian's coming over at the end of the month to fish with us for a few days; Bill and I thought it would be fun to have you and Carol join us."

"Brian," I knew, meant Brian Chan, my co-author on *Morris & Chan on Fly Fishing Trout Lakes* and as much a fly-fishing luminary in Canada as anyone is in the States. This was too good to miss—good friends and fine fishing. Carol and I would work it out.

When I called Peter back to tell him we were coming, I recalled Mike's comments on Slough Creek about the fly cutthroats "hardly ever ignore" and asked, "Should I bring a lot of Chernobyl Ants?"

"Well, I've heard of the fly, but we've never heard about it doing anything special up here. I wouldn't bother with it."

I tied up a bunch anyway. As I said, Mike knows his fishing, and cutthroats are cutthroats, wherever they are.

When we got there it was plain hot, shirt-soaking breath-stealing hot. Carol and I soon figured out that the only escape was to wade bare-legged in the cool, cobble-bottomed rivers, and that felt divine.

Shortly after we had arrived at our bed and breakfast, Peter told me over the phone, "We had some guys up here last week who just cleaned up with Chernobyl Ants. Did you bring some?"

"Yea," I replied, "and I brought my tying suitcase too. I'll get to work on 'em." Every morning that week I tied a half to a full dozen Ants. Peter fished them. I fished them. Carol fished them. Brian fished them. Brian's daughter, Carlyn, fished them. Bill fished them. We tried other flies—nymphs, dry flies, big and small—and nothing seemed to draw the cutthroats up through three, six, ten, even twelve feet of streamy, golden flow nearly so consistently as a big, black Chernobyl Ant.

On the third day, eating lunch in the shade, I said, "I just can't believe how these fish go for the Ant—it's weird!"

A faint grin curled the edges of Peter's mouth. "Yea," he said, "that fly I told you not to bother with."

1. Start the thread at the hook's bend. Cut a strip of closed-cell foam sheeting about as wide as half the length of the hook's shank. Trim one end of the strip to rounded.

2. Bind the strip over the bend with a collar of *firm* thread-turns (not tight turns—tight turns can cut foam). The rounded end of the strip should project over and just beyond the bend.

3. Double a length of rubber-strand over the thread; then slide the strand down to the thread collar and bind it there. Bind another strand on the opposite side in this same manner.

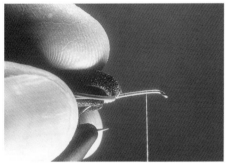

4. Draw back the foam and strands, and then advance the thread up the shank in close, tight turns to about three quarters up the shank.

5. Lower the foam-strip and build another thread collar over it about three quarters up the shank. Bind a short length of rubber-strand on each side as before.

6. Cut a slim strip of yellow foam for a strike indicator. Bind the strip atop the second thread collar. Trim its ends fairly short. The yellow should appear only as two bright stub-ends. Trim the front end of the black foam strip to a short, rounded head, extending past the hook's eye a little.

7. Trim the legs to length, which should be slightly long—at least a full hook-length—to make them appear gangly. That completes this bizarre new fly with which cutthroats seem so taken. (Though friends assure me that browns and rainbows go for it, too.)

Nymphs

*A still-alive chironomid pupa,
suctioned from the throat of a trout.*

Smooth meadow streams like this one can be fine places to fish a nymph.

Skip releases a nymph-caught rainbow.

Brook trout gathered in the corner of a lake.

THE FEATHER DUSTER

HOOK:	Heavy wire, 1X or 2X long, sizes 16 to 10.
THREAD:	Brown or olive 6/0 or 8/0.
TAIL:	For size-12 hooks and larger, pheasant-tail fibers. For size-14 hooks and smaller, partridge fibers.
RIB:	Fine copper wire.
BODY:	Natural ostrich herl.
WING CASE and LEGS:	For size-12 hooks and larger, pheasant-tail fibers. For size-14 hooks and smaller, partridge fibers.

You'd think a professional writer, one who has pored over dictionaries, style guides, thesauruses, and works of the acknowledged literary masters of prose, all in pursuit of the right word, could give a new fly a good name. But, alas, I'm lousy at it.

Which is why I'm always impressed with a name that rises, from among the tangle of featureless gray fly names, and sparkles. I'm impressed with the name "Feather Duster"; it sparkles. Vividly it captures its object's essence.

The Feather Duster itself does not sparkle. It is a fuzzy gray-brown nymph composed of what appear to be the same fuzzy gray-brown fibers used in an actual household feather duster.

Wally Eagle created the Feather Duster, and gave the fly its herl body because, according to *Fly Patterns of Yellowstone*, by Mathews and Juracek, he "has never liked to dub."

The book describes the Feather Duster as an imitation of a mayfly nymph, but adds that it "can also suggest damselfly, dragonfly, and little stonefly nymphs."

It is, in a nutshell, a distinctive nymph with a fine record for persuading western trout.

And, of course, it's got one of those infuriatingly fresh, expressive names that seem always just beyond my grasp.

1. Start the thread on the hook's shank. Wind some lead wire over the front half of the shank, cut the ends of the lead, and then bind it. Build a little dubbing of any kind at both ends of the lead.

Bind on a few pheasant-tail or partridge fibers at the hook's bend. Bind on some copper wire at the bend. Trim the ends of both the fibers and wire.

2. Snip off the very tips of three to five ostrich herls. Bind the herls by their cut tips at the hook's bend.

Cut a thin section of pheasant-tail or partridge-flank fibers and keep the tips of the fibers even. Bind the fibers atop the center of the shank. The fibers should project back a full hook's length. Trim and bind the fibers' butts.

3. Bind the tips of the wing-case fibers at the hook's eye with a couple of light thread-turns. Wind the herls forward to the wing-case fibers. Back off the turns of thread holding down the fibers. Tug the fibers back and continue winding the herls to just behind the hook's eye. Secure them there with tight thread-turns and then trim the butts closely.

4. Wind the copper wire forward in seven to ten open spirals to the hook's eye. Secure the wire there with tight thread-turns; then trim the wire closely.

5. Draw the wing-case fibers forward and down. Bind them there just behind the eye.

6. Draw three to five fiber-tips back along each side of the hook and bind them there. Trim away any remaining fiber-tips. Build and complete a thread head.

THE ZEBRA MIDGE

HOOK:	Heavy wire, 2X long (Ken prefers a hook with a humped shank), sizes 20 to 10.
THREAD:	Black 8/0 or 6/0.
ABDOMEN:	Two strands of fly-line backing—one strand is colored black, red, or gray; the other is left its original white. Another combination is a yellow strand with a black one.
THORAX:	Black dubbing (any kind).

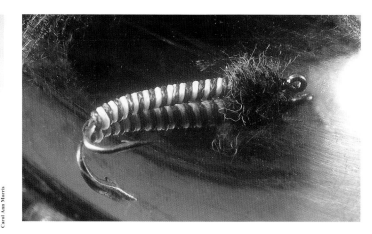

Carol Ann Morris

My friend Ken Fujii, a trout-lake fisherman of the first order, created the Zebra Midge. He lets it sink deep under its own weight, below a strike indicator and a floating line, and then gives the fly plenty of rest and only an occasional slow, short draw.

Chironomids are a standard feed for trout in most lakes, and the Zebra imitates the chironomid's "pupal" stage, that form of the insect that leaves the bottom-muck, and then rises in its awk-ward squirming to the surface. Soon it leaves the water in its winged, adult stage. Rivers have lots of chironomids too, and the Zebra should be just as effective on them as it is on lakes. There is never a bad time to fish an imitation chironomid in any trout water—the real ones hatch year round.

I've fished a slow, deep Zebra Midge to some very difficult trout in a hard-fished private pond, a pond that had proved to be an acid test for any trout fly. It passed that test, repeatedly.

1. Snip two sections from some fly-line backing, each a few inches long. Color one strand with a permanent marking pen; leave the other white.

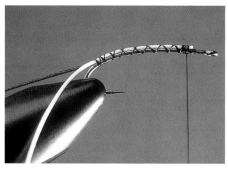

2. Start the thread about 1/8-inch back from the hook's eye. There, bind the ends of the two strands of fly-line backing. Spiral the thread tightly down the backing and the hook's shank to partway down its bend. Spiral the thread back up to its starting point.

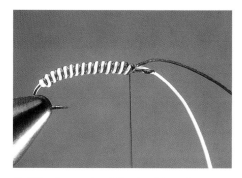

3. Trim the ends of the backing, if necessary. Wind the two strands of backing together up the shank to about 1/8-inch back from the hook's eye. The strands should lie flat, their colors staggered in a tight candy-cane pattern. Bind the ends of the strands and then trim them.

4. Dub a short, full thorax.

5. Build a small thread-head, whip finish and trim the thread, and add head cement to complete the Zebra Midge.

6. This photo shows two Zebra Midges, one small, one large, each lying on the strands from which its abdomen was formed. The strands for the small Zebra are size-A rod-winding thread. Use whatever strand material forms a slim body on the hook size you've chosen.

BIRD'S STONEFLY NYMPH

HOOK:	Heavy wire, 3X long, sizes 10 to 4.
THREAD:	Orange 8/0, 6/0, or 3/0.
WEIGHT:	Lead wire.
TAILS:	Brown-dyed goose biots.
RIB:	Orange floss or heavy thread.
ABDOMEN:	Brown muskrat fur or brown-dyed rabbit fur.
WING CASE:	Dark mottled turkey primary or brown-dyed teal.
LEGS:	A furnace or brown saddle hackle.
THORAX:	Peacock herl.

If Terry Hellekson's comments on page 73 of his book *Popular Fly Patterns* formed your introduction to the Bird's Stonefly Nymph, you might have the wrong impression. Hellekson's book was published in 1976, and in it he describes this fly as an "old" pattern. It would be easy to assume that by 1996 the Bird's Stonefly Nymph had become but a memory.

Simply not so. Age, it seems, has little effect on some fly patterns, and the Bird's Stonefly Nymph proves it by continuing to appear in the catalogs of fly companies, the bins of fly shops, anglers' fly boxes, and the mouths of stonefly-seeking trout.

It should surprise no one familiar with the Bird's Stonefly Nymph that it has held its own all these years—it's just the sort of good-looking fly that fly fishers like to see in their boxes, and its orange rib, peacock thorax, and neatly split tails make it a fine imitation of the nymph of the huge western stonefly commonly known as the salmonfly.

A word of caution, the name is often shortened to Bird's Stonefly or just Bird's Stone. Since there is also a dry fly called Bird's Stonefly Adult or Bird's Stonefly Dry, the shortened title for the nymph can cause confusion.

The "Bird's" in Bird's Stonefly Nymph refers to its creator Cal Bird, a commercial artist living in California when he developed the fly in the early 1960s.

A real salmonfly nymph.

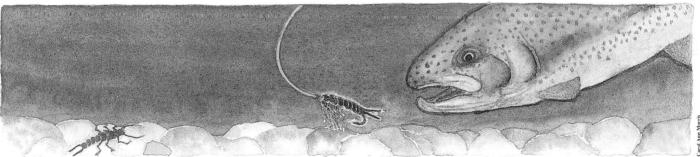

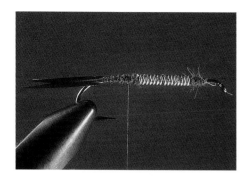

1. Start the thread near the hook's bend and then bind a goose biot on each side of the shank—these biot tails should be at least as long as the hook's gape is wide. Wrap lead wire from one third up the shank to 1/8-inch short of the hook's eye. Trim the ends of the wire, bind the wire with thread-turns, and then taper its ends with a little dubbing.

2. Bind some floss or heavy thread at the rear of the shank, for the rib (I use two strands of flat waxed nylon). Dub a full, tapered abdomen to slightly past halfway up the shank.

3. Wind the floss or thread up the abdomen in five to seven ribs. (I use two strands of flat waxed nylon and twist them together before wrapping them as a rib.) Bind the rib at the front of the abdomen with tight thread-turns and then trim off the end of the rib material.

4. Bind a section of turkey primary over the thorax area, projecting back over the abdomen. The section should be about as wide as the hook's gape.

5. Bind a hackle by its tip or butt (both are acceptable but create different effects) at the rear of the thorax area. Bind three to five full peacock herls at the same place.

6. Spin the herls lightly around the thread. Wind this thread-herl rope up the thorax-area to just back from the hook's eye. Separate out the ends of the the herl and bind them there tightly. Trim off the ends of the herl.

7. Wind the hackle up the herl-thorax in four to six open spirals. Secure the end of the hackle just back from the hook's eye with tight thread-turns. Trim the hackle's stem closely.

8. Either trim the hackle fibers from the top of the thorax or draw those fibers down the sides of the thorax. Draw the turkey section up and forward; then bind it just behind the hook's eye. Trim the end of the section closely, build a tapered thread head, whip finish the thread, trim the thread, and then add head cement to the head.

THE HALFBACK

HOOK:	Heavy wire, 1X to 3X long, sizes 12 to 8.
THREAD:	Black 6/0 or 8/0.
TAIL:	Pheasant-rump or pheasant-tail fibers.
ABDOMEN:	Peacock herl.
WING CASE and LEGS:	The same kind of fibers used in the tail.
THORAX:	Peacock herl.

The Fullback

Carol Ann Morris

They are a set, so close in form that one can always substitute for the other. They are the Canadian nymphs, the Fullback and the Halfback. The difference between them is slight—some feather fibers over the abdomen of the Fullback, none on the Halfback.

Though the Halfback and Fullback are considered lake flies, they would certainly be good in streams. But my impression is that Canadians seldom give them a chance there.

Few Canadian fly fishers would go to a trout lake without a couple of Halfbacks and Fullbacks on hand, at least a couple. If not a full dozen.

1. These are two types of pheasant fibers you can use for the tail in the Halfback: pheasant *tail* (on the left) and pheasant *rump* (on the right).

2. Start the thread on the hook's shank, and then bind on four to eight pheasant fibers at the hook's bend. The resulting tail should be one half to two thirds the shank's length. Bind three to five peacock herls at the hook's bend. Twist the herls and thread together, and then wind the resulting herl-rope halfway up the shank.

3. Separate out the herls and thread. Bind the herls there, and then trim their ends off. Even the tips of another bunch of pheasant. Bind the fibers at mid-shank, tips back. The fibers should extend back, from where they are bound, about one full hook's length. Trim the butts of the fibers.

4. Bind on and wrap a few more herls, as before. Bind and trim the herls just slightly back from the hook's eye—no further back then the length of the eye itself.

5. Pull the pheasant fibers forward and down. Bind them firmly behind the eye.

6. Pull the fibers' tips down and back and bind them there, beneath the hook.

I prefer to divide the tips to the sides, and then bind them there. The completed fly at the top of this page has the fiber-tip legs arranged as I like them.

THE GRAY NYMPH

HOOK: Heavy wire, regular shank or 1X long, sizes 16 to 6.

THREAD: Gray 8/0 or 6/0.

TAIL: Same fibers as used for the hackle.

BODY: Muskrat.

HACKLE: Grizzly hen-saddle or hen-neck hackle.

"Gray Nymph," the man replied. But you'd have to know the question that preceded his answer to understand why I was—why we all were—listening closely. This was the question: "What fly are you using?" It might also help you to know that while the Gray Nymph man was catching trout after trout from the small Central Oregon lake, the three of us were catching nothing. Then the man with the Gray Nymphs passed a few around. We tied them to our tippets, cast them out on full-sinking lines, and were soon busy catching fish of our own...with a new respect for this venerable old fly pattern.

There isn't much to the Gray Nymph—a tail, a hackle, a fuzzy body—but it's a good bet fished dead drift along a streambed; twitched in front of trout rising in streams or lakes; and, of course, fished on a sinking line well down in trout lakes.

The Gray Nymph was created by Dee Vissing.

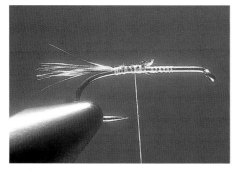

1. Start the thread on the hook's shank; then strip some fibers from the side of a grizzly hackle and bind them as a tail. This tail should be about half to three quarters the length of the shank.

2. Wind some lead or lead-substitute wire over the forward half of the shank; (leave some space behind the hook's eye, as shown). Cut the ends of the wire closely. Bind the wire with tight thread-turns.

3. Dub a full, tapered body of muskrat fur up about three quarters of the shank.

4. Strip the long, fluffy fibers from the base of a grizzly hackle. Bind the hackle by its stem just behind the eye. Wind the thread back over the stem to the front of the body, a distance of only about 1/16 of an inch. Trim off the hackle's stem.

5. Clamp the tip of the hackle in hackle pliers; then wind the hackle back towards the body in three or four turns. Let the pliers hang. Spiral the thread tightly forward through the hackle to the eye. Find and trim out the hackle's tip.

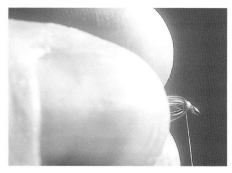

6. Draw back the hackle fibers. Build a tapered thread head; then whip finish the thread, trim its end, and coat the head with head cement to complete the Gray Nymph.

THE ROYAL FLUSH

HOOK:	Heavy wire, 1X long (standard nymph hook), humped shank is optional, sizes 16 to 10.
BEAD:	Gold metal, 3/32-inch for size-16 hooks, 7/64-inch for size-14, and 1/8-inch for size-12 and -10.
WEIGHT:	Lead or lead-substitute wire, 0.015-inch (could go larger on the bigger hooks). Lead is optional.
THREAD:	Black or red 6/0 or 8/0. (Try the red sometime—kicks up the brightness factor a solid notch.)
TAIL:	Golden pheasant tippets.
RIB:	Fine red copper wire over red Flashabou.
ABDOMEN:	Two or three peacock herls.
WING CASE:	Clear Stretch Flex, Scud Back, or Medallion sheeting, 1/8-inch wide (this clear strip is optional), over white duck primary, goose shoulder, or any white feather-section.
THROAX:	Same peacock herl used for the abdomen.
HACKLE:	Brown hen neck, as a half-collar.

The Royal Coachman dry fly stands as the flagship for all "attractor" fly patterns, flies designed not so much to imitate fish food as to satisfy flights of the imagination. Some would argue that no one fly that can represent all the attractors with their broad range from elegant to quirky, but if there is one, it must be the Royal Coachman. It tops the list in many respects. It's as plush as any fly: a body composed of two shining collars of peacock herl separated by a band of rich red floss, chestnut hackle, snowy white wings, and the most intriguing tail of pheasant tippets—a bundle of orange-gold stalks tipped like cattails with velvety black fuzz. And the Royal Coachman is well known to any serious fly fisher, a fly with (my impression) an unmatched record of popularity and (fact) a record of over a hundred years of catching trout. So I had no qualms about using it as a the model for my Royal Flush nymph.

The two, however, are different flies indeed. For starters, one floats, one sinks. And there are other differences. After some experimentation I eliminated the Coachman's floss band altogether from my fly, but echoed it with a red rib of brilliant Flashabou reinforced with red copper wire—the banded effect was just too unnatural for my sensibilities. Then there's that great, round golden bead on the head of my nymph—no Royal Coachman in the pattern's century-long reign ever sported such a thing.

But otherwise, the Royal Coachman's influence on my Royal Flush is consistent: brown hackle, pheasant-tippet tail, and even an outlandish white wing case in place of the Coachman's outlandish white wings.

Fanciful as it clearly is, the Royal Flush is arguably not entirely unnatural. The mayfly *Ameletus's* three nymphal tails are tipped with contrasting color along the lines of the Royal Flush's golden pheasant tippet, though the pattern is reversed in the mayfly—dark shafts with light tips. And the white wing case in my fly could remind trout of a whitish nymph having just shed an exoskeleton, as mayflies do numerous times throughout their underwater lives. The dark and shining herl body is a long-proven approach to artificial nymph design, as is the brown hackle half-collar. Still, nothing is going to explain away that golden bead.

But probably nothing should. Nymphs with gold beads catch a lot of trout, as do fanciful attractor flies in general.

Perhaps attractor flies work precisely *because* they look unlike anything a fish ever ate. No one knows for sure. But attractors do work, sometimes far better than solid imitations.

To date, I've fished my Royal Flush strictly in streams—and it's often a real producer there. Technique is nothing special—the fly riding deep, dead-drifted below a strike indicator, a full-floating line behind that. Sometimes I use my nymph when there is no hatch to unify the trout's purpose, and sometimes on the whim that a bright, plush, shining little fly the fish have never before seen will pique their interest.

The Royal Flush should be a solid attractor fly in trout lakes, but I have yet to test that theory.

The name Royal Flush comes from a winning hand in poker (the "Royal" serving also as a tip of the hat to its ancestor). Seemed appropriate.

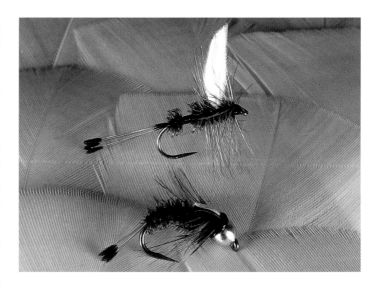

The Royal Flush and its ancestor, the Royal Coachman dry fly.

TYING STRATEGIES

I like to double a strand of the Flashabou so that *two* ends project from the hook's bend—Flashabou is tough enough for a temporary rib (it is soon reinforced with wire), but a heavy hand or a swipe across the hook's point can part it; the second end is a back-up. Nowadays it is common to strengthen peacock-herl bodies by twisting the herls with the thread. Not necessary with the Royal Flush, though—the counter-wrapped wire rib gives the herl plenty of reinforcement.

An alternate way to tie the Royal Flush is to dub tightly against the rear of the wing-case materials with just a *little* dubbing

(then dub a little out into the thorax to smooth things out) so the materials stand straight up. Then bind on the herls at the bead, wind the herls down the full length of the hook's shank to the bend, and then secure the herls by wrapping the Flashabou all the way up to the bead in ribs. Right away, wind the copper wire over the Flashabou and up the body; then everything is secure. This is a tricky approach because the wing-case materials may not be all that keen on staying upright, and the Flashabou is a bit fragile for securing all the herls, even temporarily. But once you get the hang of this method you'll find it fast and neat. Try it.

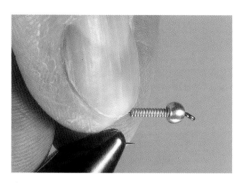

1. Slide the bead, small end of the hole forward, up the hook's shank to its eye. Mount the hook in your vise, and then wrap a layer of lead (if you want lead) up the full length of the shank. Cut the ends of the lead close. Push the lead up firmly into the rear of the bead. The lead and bead will now cover about two thirds to three quarters of the shank.

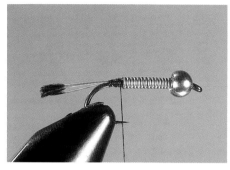

2. Start the thread directly behind the lead windings. Bind a small bunch of pheasant tippets atop the shank, at the hook's bend, as a tail. The tail should be half to two thirds the length of the shank. Wind the thread up the fibers and shank to the rear of the lead. Trim off the butts of the fibers closely, so they lie right up against the lead.

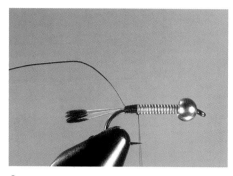

3. Bind some fine red copper wire from the rear of the lead windings to the bend. Trim off the stub-end of the wire, if necessary. (You are trying to fill the gap behind the lead for a smooth under-body, so try to keep your materials bound right behind the lead but up *against* the lead.)

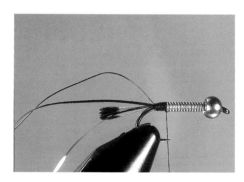

4. Double a full length of red Flashabou over the thread. Bind the doubled end against the rear of the lead and then down to the tail.

5. Trim the last half-inch or so off the tips of three peacock herls (you can use two for small hooks). Bind the herls by their cut tips in the space behind the lead windings (remember—fill the gap, smooth things out). Spiral the thread to *slightly* past halfway to the rear of the bead. Wind the three herls together halfway up the shank—toward you over the top and away from you beneath the hook, the opposite of the usual direction—and then bind them there, but don't cut them.

6. Advance the thread over the ends of the herls a couple of turns; then pull the butts of the herls firmly back along one side of the hook and bind them. (As an alternate, you could just trim off the herls now, and then bind new ones on later for the thorax. You'll soon see what I mean.) At the middle of the shank between the rear of the bead and the tail, bind a strip of clear Stretch Flex or the like. Atop the clear strip bind a section of white duck primary or such. The section should be slightly slimmer than the hook's gape. Trim the butts of these wing-case materials and then bind them thoroughly.

7. Spiral the thread to the rear of the bead. Wind the remaining herl to the rear of the bead (in reverse direction, again). Bind the herl there. Trim the ends of the herl closely.

8. Pull the wing-case materials up and forward; then bind them (temporarily) with one or two light turns of thread. Wind the Flashabou in three to five turns to the rear of the wing-case materials—in the normal direction, away from you over the top and towards you below. Back off the thread to release the wing case stuff, and then continue winding the Flashabou to the bead in two or three turns.

9. Bind the end of the Flashabou; then trim it off. If all went well, trim off the second, back-up, strand at the bend.

Bind the wing-case materials temporarily again. Wind the wire over the Flashabou, tightly, right in its tracks, to the wing case. Free the wing-case materials and then continue the wire up to the rear of the bead. Bind the wire. Trim the ends of both wire and Flashabou.

10. Find a hen hackle appropriate to the size of your hook using a hackle gauge. Strip the hackle's base, and then bind the hackle by its bare stem up against the rear of the bead. The body of the hackle should project forward, off the hook's eye. Wind the thread back in about three close turns. Trim off the hackle's stem.

11. Wind the hackle back in three close turns, then wind the thread *forward*, *through* the fibers to the bead. This makes a very strong hackle collar—its stem is crossed and reinforced by thread three times.

12. Pinch down the hackle fibers firmly, so they sweep back.

13. Part the hackle fibers on top, and then pull the white duck-section forward and down. Bind the section against the rear of the bead. Pull the Stretch Flex strip forward and down atop the duck, and then bind it atop the duck. Trim the ends of the duck and Stretch Flex closely. Whip finish and trim the thread. Add head cement to the whip finish to complete the Royal Flush.

THE MONTANA STONE

HOOK:	Heavy wire, 3X or 4X long, sizes 10 to 6.
WEIGHT:	Lead or lead-substitute wire.
THREAD:	Black 8/0, 6/0, or 3/0.
TAIL:	Black hackle fibers.
ABDOMEN:	Black chenille, thick enough to provide fullness. (The fly in the photos has thick chenille; some would prefer thinner.)
WING CASE:	Black chenille, doubled, same thickness as that used in the abdomen.
LEGS:	One black hackle. Its fibers should be soft and webby and two thirds the length of the hook's shank.
THORAX:	Yellow chenille, same thickness as the black.

After presenting my case for the Montana Stone as a subject for my column, I added that I'd been surprised during my speaking tour in Sweden to find that the fly was huge over there. "I *know*," replied my editor's familiar voice from the telephone reciever, "and it's just as big in England. Let me send you a copy of a English catalog that lists all kinds of Montana Stones."

I let him, of course. Writers usually let their editors do whatever they please, other than mangling copy or paying late.

Sure enough, the foggy copies listed the "Montana," as it's sometimes called, in seven variations, three of which where available on two different hook styles. Five of the variations dealt with color only—standard black-and-yellow, olive, red, white, and orange—and the other two were "Montanabous," one lime, the other in pearl, which looked to have marabou tails.

Indeed, Europe has discovered the Montana Nymph. In the States it's old news, but good news.

This fly has been around since at least the early 1970s. During the seventies it probably reached its height of popularity—it seemed everyone was throwing Montanas into western rivers. And since everyone was catching trout, they continued to throw them.

The Montana Stone remains a solid and popular stonefly-nymph imitation. It is usually tied on big hooks, to imitate big stoneflies, most notably the giant salmonfly. But it's sometimes on smaller hooks. I don't know what the Europeans imitate with it, but they probably use it simply because it catches trout, and the trout probably take it simply because it looks alive and corpulent.

My collection of fly-pattern books fails to name the originator of the Montana Stone. Well, whoever came up with it, he or she did it right.

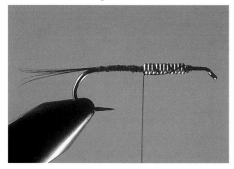

1. Start the thread on the hook's shank. Wind some lead wire up the shank. Trim the ends of the wire; then bind it with tight thread-turns. Bind hackle fibers atop the hook's bend as a tail.

2. Bind some chenille along the shank to the hook's bend. Advance the thread. Wind the chenille forward to just past mid-shank; bind, then trim, the end of the chenille.

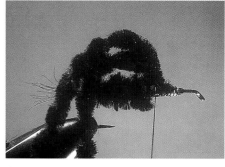

3. Double a short length of chenille and bind its ends at the front of the abdomen, atop the hook.

4. Strip the fuzzy fibers from the base of a hackle, and then bind that hackle at the front of the abdomen.

5. Bind the end of some yellow chenille at the front of the abdomen. Advance the thread. Wind the yellow chenille to the hook's eye; bind it, and trim the chenille.

6. Spiral the hackle up the chenille in three or four turns; bind, then trim, the hackle's tip. Draw the loop of chenille forward over the thorax, as a wing case, bind it, trim it. Build a thread head.

EGG FLIES

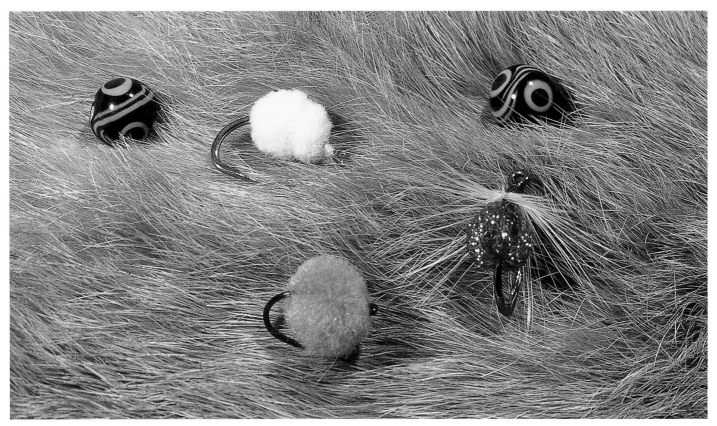

Strange spherical creatures cast their solemn gaze over a trio of fine egg-imitating flies.

I have fished egg flies on only two occasions, but on both, the results were impressive.

My first time out with these flies was on a shallow ribbon of a river on Alaska's Kodiak Island. Silver salmon swarmed in the lagoon at the river's mouth, and it would have been easy to just spend the whole week there teasing the big fish with streamers and stout, floating hair-flies. But I knew there were dolly varden char up in the runs and pools seeking loose eggs from the spawning crowds of salmon, and the river looked good. So, blowing madly and often on my screeching bear whistle and watching always for those unpredictable residents I was hoping not to surprise, who also had keen interest in the salmon, I made my way cautiously up the river's calm estuary into its wide, fresh flow. I learned quickly that all I needed to do was toss a little egg fly out wherever the current picked up and was at least calf-deep, let it drift to the bottom—if it got that far—and then watch one or more dollies rush at it in the clear water. They were small fish, mostly twelve inches to two pounds—though we caught them up to five—but just to get to my fly they slammed through the heavy salmon, startling them to flight.

I tried other flies—dry flies, streamers, nymphs, and "flesh flies," nothing more than tan fur on the hide bound to hooks, to suggest flesh chunks from the bodies of dead salmon. None worked. Not to say that none worked as well as the egg flies the dollies charged with abandon—nothing else worked at *all*, nothing else hooked even a single fish. But whenever I switched back to a single-egg imitation, back came the greedy dollies.

I was impressed.

Two years later I fished an egg fly again, this time in a substantial beaver pond in Idaho. My friends Mike and Doug—dedicated young fly fishers who knew plenty of local secrets—had taken me and my wife Carol there to, if nothing else, show us that trout in beaver ponds can grow big. They made their point.

They told us that egg flies were best, but also told us they had no idea why. We just threw the flies out, let them drift lazily down, watched our leaders for a sign. I got such a sign, struck, felt something briefly, then nothing. Then Mike hooked a fish and lost it, and it was clearly large. Soon he hooked another and, eventually, landed it. Seven pounds, we judged it, seven pounds of pink-banded rainbow trout. And it had taken an egg fly.

That's the range of my egg-fly experience in full. Not extensive, but certainly promising.

To make this article right, however, I needed help from someone who has fished egg flies a lot. So I went to Jim Kerr, a fly-fishing guide and once co-owner of Port Townsend Angler, a fly shop in the little town on Washington's Olympic Peninsula for which it was named. Jim often fishes and guides fly fishers for steelhead on the rivers of the Peninsula's west side. And frequently does so with egg flies.

VARIATIONS ON THE GLO-BUG

While the standard approach for tying a Glo-Bug of medium size or larger is to use four strands of yarn, Jim prefers only two strands. "It's not as dense this way," he explained, "but it's more translucent."

One he tied for me had lead barbell eyes in it's center, the securing thread-turns for the yarn angling all in one direction across the canted stem of the eyes. Glo-Bugs tied this way, he said, are now quite common on Peninsula rivers, and can be deadly for steelhead when fished below a strike indicator.

There are other ways to tie a fly that imitates a fish egg. Ted Leeson's Krystal Egg series is one. Another is to wind chenille up into a large ball on the hook's shank, the Iliamna Pinkie. We'll look at both of these too.

Fishing an egg fly in a trout stream even when no fish are spawning and, consequently, no fish eggs are present can sometimes be deadly effective.

I knew that the standard egg-fly fly pattern—often called a "Glo-Bug" or "Roe Bug"—is tied on a hook of heavy to very heavy wire with a very short shank, and that the egg part of the fly is just a special synthetic yarn bound in one place and then trimmed, strategically, with (theoretically) a single snip of the scissors. But I didn't know some of the newest Glo-Bug variations. Jim, however, did.

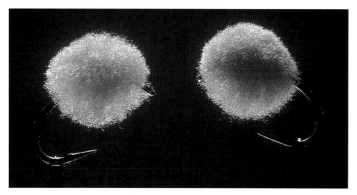

The Glo-Bug on the left was tied with only two strands of yarn, consequently it is less dense and more translucent than the fony-strand Glo-Bug on the right.

WHEN TO FISH AN EGG FLY

Jim says that fish relish fish eggs and tend to take them whenever the little spheres of protein appear. That makes sense—a substantial ball of sustenance that can neither fly away nor swim off is an easy and worthwhile target. He has seen steelhead, trout, char, and even whitefish focus on fish eggs, sometimes to the point that only an egg fly would produce. So the question of when to fish an egg fly has an obvious answer—fish one whenever fish eggs are free in the water, which would, of course, normally be when some species of fish is spawning. But as my friends in Idaho proved, egg flies can be good even when real fish eggs aren't present. Perhaps the fish move to an isolated egg out of instinct, or because they've had eggs before and liked them; no one can say for certain. But it's a fact that egg flies sometimes produce when nothing is spawning, and that's just the way fish can be.

SIZES AND COLORS

The simplest way to determine the right size of egg fly for the moment is to find a sample and match it. Finding a sample isn't always practical, so the next choice is to make a reasonable guess, and then test it with the fish. The eggs of silver salmon, for example, are larger than the eggs of trout, similar to the relative difference in size of the fishes themselves. But what experienced fly fisher hasn't seen fish prefer outsize flies? Perhaps a Black Wulff tied on a big size-8 hook taking trout after trout when a diminutive size-18 parachute—just right to match the PMD mayflies speckling the surface of the stream—is consistently ignored. For whatever reason, fish don't always want a fly of appropriate size—egg flies included—so it's always reasonable to show them too-large and too-small egg flies and just see what happens.

Color in an egg fly can be critical, Jim says. He's often seen steelhead move only to egg flies of orange...or pink, or red, or even black.

Black?

Yes, he insists, an all-black egg fly can sometimes work wonders on steelhead, and I believe him. Let us just say that the whims of fish are often beyond the understanding of man, and let it go at that.

Most Glo-Bug egg flies have a spot of a contrasting color.

Neither fish nor fisherman seems to worry much about what color that spot is, just so long as the results look good. And it's likely that an egg fly without a spot is just as productive as one with a spot. Still, the spot does look good...

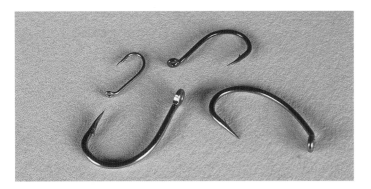

ABOUT EGG-FLY HOOKS

Egg flies are normally tied on hooks designed just for egg flies. Such hooks are marketed under names like "Glo-Bug hook," "egg-fly hook," and so on. Manufacturers seem to agree that an egg-fly hook has very stout wire and a very short, curved shank. What they can't seem to agree on is size—two supposed size-8 egg hooks from different manufacturers may be entirely different in shank length and gape. Bear this in mind when you consider the hook sizes listed in the patterns that follow.

I have also had good success with egg flies tied on the tightly curved scud-emerger hooks and even on short-shank nymph hooks.

EGG-FLY PATTERNS

Here are three fly patterns for egg-imitating flies. Leeson's Krystal Egg is clearly the most radical, but it is hardly news to old-hand fly fishers that raising the shine-factor beyond Mother Nature's range can sometimes make a fly more effective.

ILIAMNA PINKIE

HOOK:	Heavy wire, short shank, sizes 8 and 6.
THREAD:	White.
WEIGHT:	Lead wire under the body, optional.
BODY:	Pink, orange, red, cream, or yellow chenille built up to a ball.
COMMENTS:	Very simple. About the only thing that can go wrong with this fly is for the chenille to topple and loosen. Wrapping the chenille tightly usually eliminates this problem.

KRYSTAL EGG   *Ted Leeson*

HOOK:	Heavy wire, short shank, medium to large, sizes 8 and 4.
THREAD:	Six-ought, similar to the body's color.
BODY:	Krystal Flash in red, pink, orange, or chartreuse.
HACKLE:	White, large.
COMMENTS:	The best way I have found to form the egg-bulge is to bind half the Krystal Flash on the near side of the hook's shank, then bind the other half along the far side. All the strands now project back off the hook's bend. I then advance the thread to just behind the hook's eye, draw the strands straight forward and stroke them to even the pressure on them, and then push them straight back—the result is a neat, shiny ball. I continue to hold the fibers firmly as I work a few turns of thread over them with whichever hand is free for the job. The rest is obvious.

GLO-BUG   *The Bug Shop of Anderson, California*

HOOK:	Heavy wire, short shank, sizes 16 and 4.
THREAD:	Red 6/0 (or a color to blend with the yarn's color).
BODY:	Glo-Bug yarn in orange, pink, peach, red, chartreuse, and all-black.
SPOT:	A strip separated from a section of Glo-Bug yarn, a color to contrast with the main color of the egg.

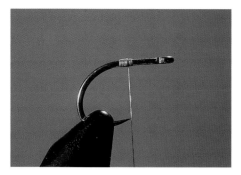

1. Start the thread at the center of the hook's shank. Trim off the end of the thread.

2. Cut two to four 1 1/2-inch sections of yarn and then hold them atop the hook, ends even. Push the yarn down so that the shank is buried in its center. Wrap several tight thread-turns around the yarn to lock it in place. The thread-turns should all be in one spot, and in about the center of the length of the yarn sections.

3. If you want a spot on the finished egg, split a slim section off some yarn of a new color; then bind it on the top or side of the previously bound sections. The section of yarn for the spot should be, at most, half the thickness of the original. (The pink yarn shown here is for the spot.)

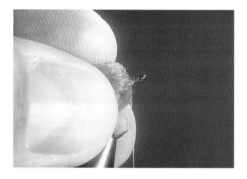

4. Stroke and then hold the yarn tightly back from the hook's eye. Pull down firmly on the thread. Pull the thread firmly forward, wind a few tight turns of it on the shank, and then whip finish it right in front of the yarn. Trim the thread.

5. Pull all the yarn straight up and hold it there firmly. Slip your scissors' blades in around the yarn. Most tiers cut too far from the hook's shank and wind up with a gargantuan egg completely out of proportion to the hook—so cut no further away than the width of the hook's gape. (And use good—sharp—scissors.) Try to make the cut in one snip. Most tiers cut straight across, but some prefer to cut in a curve from the hook's eye to its bend.

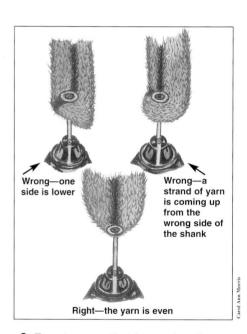

Wrong—one side is lower

Wrong—a strand of yarn is coming up from the wrong side of the shank

Right—the yarn is even

Carol Ann Morris

6. To get an egg that is round and neat, you'll need to even your tension through all the yarn. And make sure the yarn comes up level from the underside—if not, rotate it around the hook until it does. Once the tension on the yarn is consistent and the underside of the yarn is level, then you can make the scissor cut. It is also critical that, before you cut, no sections of yarn cross the underside of the hook, coming up from the wrong side.

A little care with this and your egg will be round, and won't have a tuft-tail turning the egg into a sperm.

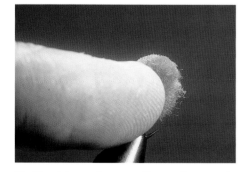

7. The trimmed yarn will now be mostly bunched atop the hook. Work it down around the underside with a few strokes of your finger tip.

If the yarn-ball is uneven (they usually are for the first few tying sessions), trim it with your scissors. But don't get carried away— Glo-Bugs should be quick to tie, since they are often quickly lost to fish or riverbeds. And fish don't seem to mind a misshapen egg.

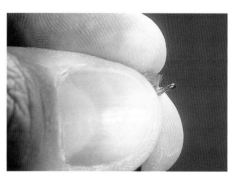

8. Mount the hook back into your vise; stroke and then hold back the trimmed yarn to expose the whip finish. Add head cement to the whip finish to complete the Glo-Bug.

THE GREEN DAMSEL

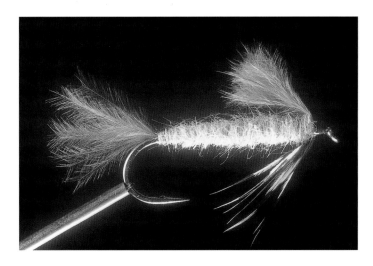

HOOK:	Heavy to standard wire, 3X long, sizes 12 to 8.
THREAD:	Olive or green 8/0 or 6/0.
TAIL:	Olive marabou.
BODY:	Pale-olive-green dubbing.
LEGS:	Fibers from any soft mottled or barred flank or breast feather—teal, mallard, guinea hen, and others—dyed pale-olive-green.
WING CASE:	Olive marabou.

Because his little book *Tying and Fishing the Fuzzy Nymphs* has been resurrected several times, from its self-published birth in 1965 to its present configuration from Stackpole Books, Polly Rosborough and his work have been continually reintroduced to fly tiers over more than three decades. Polly died recently, but because of his book, his research, and his fly patterns, he will long be remembered.

Skip's 1965 edition of Tying and Fishing the Fuzzy Nymphs.

My friend Dave Hughes, the fly-fishing author, states in *The Complete Book of Western Hatches* (with co-author Rick Hafele): "All of Rosborough's flies are works of art...." But Dave isn't the only writer to praise Polly's work. In *Nymphs*, author Earnest Schwiebert says, "Rosborough and his original research are perhaps the first major contribution to the theory and techniques of American nymph fishing since Leisenring." Terry Hellekson devotes a whole chapter of his *Popular Fly Patterns* to Rosborough and his flies; the title: "Fly Patterns of a Master." From that chapter's introduction: "...in Chiloquin, Oregon, there lives a man who is a master. He is E. H. "Polly" Rosborough, whose accomplishments in the realm of tying flies simply permit no other designation."

All this praise stems from Polly's study of western trout-stream insects and the shaggy style of nymph he developed for imitating them.

Another quote from Hughes, from a discussion on imitations of the damselfly nymph in his *Strategies for Stillwater*: "The most common dressing—and one of the best—is Polly Rosborough's Green Damsel." Which turns us from a salute to a true pioneer of fly tying to considering his justly famous fly-pattern.

A real damselfly nymph. Polly's research told him that a supple marabou tail and wing case would help his fly suggest the damsel's serpentine swimming. He was right, most fly fishers agree.

Though easy enough to tie, Polly's Green Damsel contains all the essential components of its insect model: a feathery tail; a trim, elongated body; a modest wing-case; and slim, splayed legs (although you may splay them more than Polly did if you wish; more on this later).

The nymph of the damselfly lives primarily in lakes, ponds, and other standing waters. Some very slow streams have good populations, but that's rare—the damsel has no use for currents. In late spring or summer the nymph swims up from the plant life it inhabits along a lake's bed, then, usually within a yard of the surface, levels out, and sculls its body, snakelike, towards shore.

This is the best time to fish a Green Damsel—when real damsel nymphs are migrating. And the next time you're knotting Polly's imitation onto your tippet, you might give a thought to the man who gave us the fly, along with a lot of other fine fly patterns and a fresh approach to tying flies.

1. Start the thread on the hook's shank. Bind a small bunch of marabou at the bend for a tail. I like to bind the fibers up most of the shank for an even foundation over which an even body can be formed. Trim off the butts of the fibers.

2. Dub a slim but substantial body up most of the shank, leaving just a bit of bare shank behind the hook's eye. That's how most tiers would form the body today.

Polly rolled his dubbing into what he called a "noodle," then spun that noodle tightly within a loop of tying thread, finally wrapping this loop-and-fur rope up the shank.

3. Bind a small bunch of feather fibers to the underside of the shank, as a "throat." Trim the fibers' butts. You may find this easier if you invert the hook first.

I believe the fibers better suggest the legs of a damselfly if splayed in a swept-back half-circle around the underside of the hook. But I bowed to the Master here.

4. Bind a small bunch of marabou atop the shank at the front of the body. This bunch should be slightly thicker than the one for the tail. Trim the fibers' butts, and then build and complete a thread head. Polly liked to build a long thread head of slow taper. But I've built a small head here, as is now the style.

5. Pinch and rip the marabou to a short—say, equaling the hook's gape—tail and wing-case. Add head cement to the thread head.

The surest sign that it's time to fish Polly's Green Damsel is nymphs of the damselfly crawling up on reeds and other shoreline plants to "hatch"—that is, split and escape their outermost skins, expand the wings they've carried for so long in humps on their backs, and fly off.

THE GREEN DAMSEL **43**

SCUD FLIES

"Scuds," little freshwater crustaceans that look so much like shrimp that Canadians simply refer to them *as* shrimp, are underrated trout food. They get only a fraction of the attention fly fishers give mayflies and caddis, probably because they are less common than these fellow invertebrates in streams, the classic troutwater. But scuds are particularly common—and often abundant— in lakes. And, generally, the richer a lake is in dragonflies, leeches, and other creatures trout eat, the more heavily scuds outweigh those other creatures—in other words, a relatively sterile lake may contain few or no scuds, while a rich lake may be so crowded with them that there seems room for little else. Some rich, slower-moving streams are full of scuds too. Point is, if you fish for trout, you will eventually find them focused on scuds, so you'd better have flies that imitate scuds and the knowledge to fish those flies effectively.

Real scuds.

A lot of scud-imitating flies look very similar; which you'd expect since they are all designed off the same model. But trout flies imitating one particular creature are often surprisingly varied—consider the Parachute Adams and Thorax Dun and Comparadun, all so different, yet all are imitations of the mayfly dun. The scud, however, fits into the fly tier's game fairly neatly and thus tends to dictate how the deed will be

managed. The crustacean's smooth, clear armor-shell begs for clear-plastic sheeting, its multitude of tiny legs suggests picked-out dubbing, and its rounded segmentation is easily reproduced by winding a rib over the plastic-sheet back—and these features, predictably, are standard on scud flies. Examples of scud flies that include all or most of these features include the Bighorn Shrimp; the Yellowstone Scud; the Scud by Fred Arbona; and the Scud by Al Troth, also known as the Troth Scud.

To greater and lesser degrees, some scud-flies abandon the plastic-sheet-and-dubbing-and-rib formula. Brad Befus's Epoxy Scud includes no rib, and its back is a hard coating of epoxy glue; the old-standard Werner Shrimp out of Canada has an unribbed back of deer hair and hackle-fibers for legs; and there are yet other unconventional scud-patterns, both old and new. Still, the sheet-dubbing-rib formula probably accounts for most of the scud imitations anglers tie and fish, at least in the United States. And that's because the formula keeps catching trout.

This sluggish, fertile, weedy Oregon trout stream is typical of the sort of in which scuds flourish.

SCUD FACTS

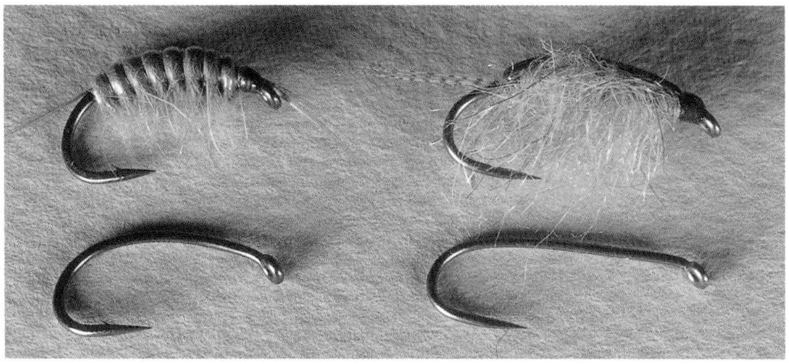

There are mayfly hatches, stonefly hatches, chironomid hatches, and others, but there are no scud hatches. While mayflies swim up through the water, loosening their outer skins, and then burst through the ceiling of a lake or river to unfurl and dry and finally rise up into the air on their new wings, scuds just putter around for a short lifetime and then die. Sounds dull to me—though they do get to mate...occasionally. Scud colors vary—grays, cream, browns, and, most commonly, olives and greens. Orange scud-flies are always popular with anglers, and are based on the orange egg sack a pregnant female scud always packs. In lakes, scuds live from the shallows to around 25 feet deep. In rivers, of course, they can live just about anywhere the current is slow enough to suit them. Water plants and debris are the scud's preferred habitat.

You've probably seen curved-shank hooks described as "scud-hooks." A lot of old hands at the scud business see this as an error—the word is, scuds only curl up when under attack, an armadillo-like defense, and spend the rest of their time swimming and resting with straightened bodies. So although the curved-shank hooks are useful (I like them for chironomid-pupa imitations, for example), I tie most of my scud flies on plain old straight-shank hooks.

FISHING A SCUD

In lakes, fishing an imitation scud is just a matter of getting the fly down near the lake's bed, where scuds live, and retrieving it slowly, with occasional pauses. If the trout are in shallow water, a floating line and weighted fly may be just fine. But in water deeper than four or five feet, I wouldn't fish a scud on anything but than a full-sinking line. Usually, that has meant a type I (slow-sinking) or type II (modestly fast-sinking) line.

In streams, the norm is to fish a scud dead drift below a strike indicator—the standard nymph-fishing-in-streams technique. But scud-streams tend to move slowly, and in the really slow water a lazy retrieve (after getting the fly down to the stream's bed) may be best.

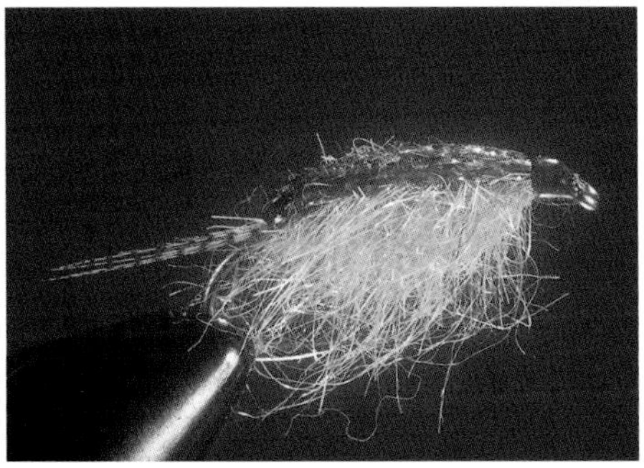

EPOXY SCUD, AMBER *Brad Befus*

HOOK: Heavy wire, 2X or 3X long, slow-curve shank, sizes 18 to 12.
THREAD: Orange 8/0 or 6/0.
TAIL: Mallard dyed wood-duck color.
BACK: Hot orange Krystal Flash, coated with epoxy glue.
BODY: Rough amber-colored dubbing, Ligas, Buggy Nymph...
EYES: Two dots from a black marking pen, under the epoxy.

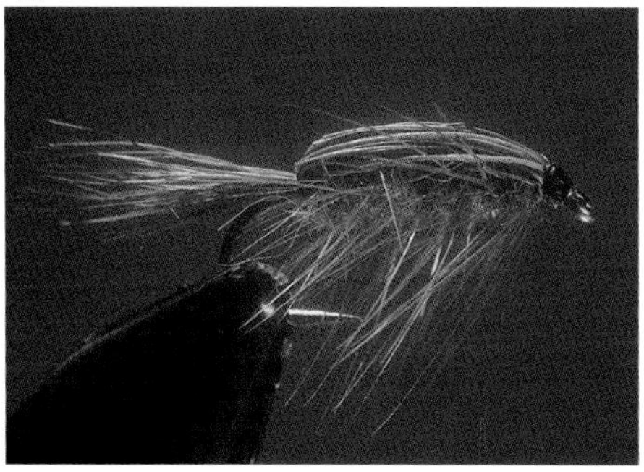

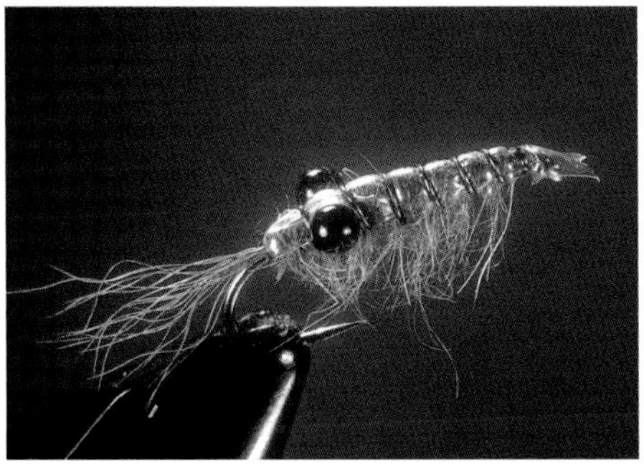

SCUD/FRESHWATER SHRIMP

HOOK: Heavy wire, humped-shank, sizes 16 to 10.
THREAD: Olive 8/0 or 6/0.
ANTENNAE: Brown calf tail and two olive Krystal Flash fibers.
EYES: Premade black barbell.
BACK: A strip cut from a plastic bag.
RIB: Fine copper wire.
BODY: Olive dubbing.

WERNER SHRIMP *Mary Stewart*

HOOK: Heavy wire, standard length to 1X long, sizes 12 to 8.
THREAD: Black or olive 8/0 or 6/0.
RIB: One brown hackle, palmered.
BODY: Olive seal or substitute.
TAIL: Natural tan-brown deer-hair tips.
BACK: Natural deer hair.

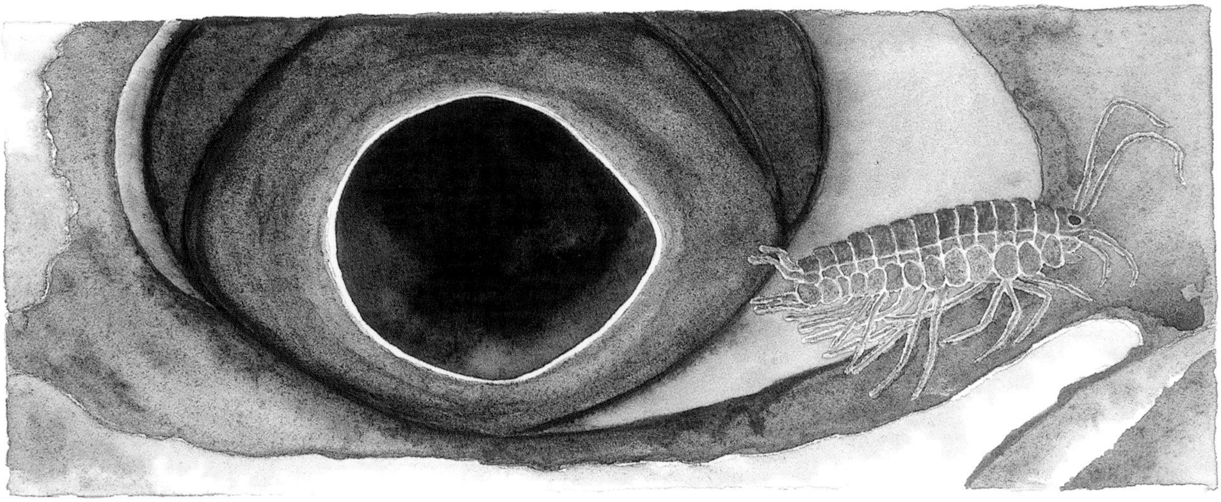
Carol Ann Morris

AL TROTH'S SCUD AND THE BIGHORN SCUD

Here are two scud-flies that are virtually one—they are, debatably, of different colors; with, also debatably, different dubbing; and their ribs (a minor feature) are of different materials. Small differences with lots of room for debate as to whether they really are differences or just overlapping variations. Nonetheless, both fly patterns are consistent producers.

TROTH and BIGHORN SCUDS

HOOK: Heavy wire, 1X long, sizes 16 to 10.

THREAD: Eight-ought or 6/0 approximating the body's color.

WEIGHT: Lead or lead-substitute wire (optional).

TAIL and ANTENNAE: Hackle fibers roughly matching the body's color (optional).

BACK: A strip of clear-plastic sheeting (as from a freezer or sandwich bag). Many now use premade strips such as Stretch Flex or Scud Back.

RIB: For Troth's Scud: fine monofilament (I use fine copper wire). For the Bighorn Shrimp: heavy thread roughly matching the body's color.

BODY: For Troth's Scud: natural fur or coarse synthetic dubbing in olive, gray, orange, brown, or cream. For the Bighorn Shrimp: fluorescent-orange or fluorescent-pink Antron dubbing.

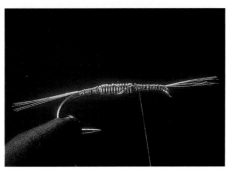

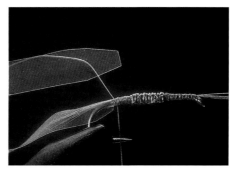

1. Start the thread on the rear third of the hook's shank; then wrap lead or lead-substitute wire over the middle third (if you want a weighted fly). Bind the lead with tight thread-turns. Bind a small bunch of hackle fibers at each end, for antennae and tail. (Many experienced scud-fishers omit the antennae and tail.)

2. Cut a strip of clear plastic from a sandwich or freezer bag. The strip should be no wider than the hook's gape, preferably a shade slimmer. Trim one tip of the strip to a blunt point. Bind the strip, by its point, on top of the hook at its bend. The photograph shows a strip cut to the proper shape and another properly bound atop the hook.

    Bind the rib material (thread, monofilament, or, as here, copper wire) at the bend.

3. Dub a fat, tapered body up the hook's shank.

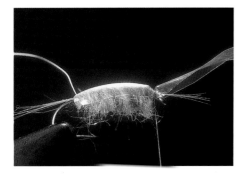

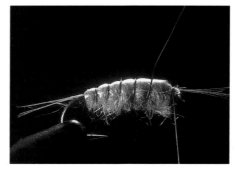

4. Pull the plastic strip up, forward, then down over the top of the body. Bind the strip just behind the hook's eye. Trim the end of the strip closely.

5. Wind the rib-material up the strip and body in six to nine ribs. Bind the rib material just behind the hook's eye; then trim it closely.

    Build a thread head, whip finish and trim the thread, add head cement to the head. When the head cement is set, use a bodkin or needle to tease out fibers from the underside of the body to form a ragged semblance of legs.

Emergers, Soft-Hackles, and a Wet Fly

Working a soft-hackled fly along the light edge of the current.

Big trout, smallish fly.

THE FOAM PMD EMERGER

HOOK:	Light wire, standard length to 1X long (standard dry-fly hook), sizes 18 and 16.
THREAD:	Yellow 8/0 or 6/0.
SHUCK:	Brown Z-lon.
ABDOMEN:	Orange-yellow beaver or rabbbit.
WING CASE:	A slim strip of gray closed-cell foam.
HACKLE:	Starling (or a pale hen-neck hackle).

"PMD" is an acronym for "Pale Morning Dun," and both are common names for a little sunny yellow mayfly that hatches from western rivers from late spring clear into fall; this long hatch-period combined with the insect's typical abundance rank the pale morning dun second only to the blue-winged olive as the great staple of western mayflies.

Craig Mathews and John Juracek's Foam PMD Emerger suggests the insect half free of its nymphal shuck and half free of the water—an awkward and vulnerable moment trout recognize as an opportunity.

Though Craig and John designed the fly for their home waters in and around Yellowstone Park, their Foam PMD Emerger is a solid choice for PMD hatches whenever and wherever you find them.

1. Start the thread on the hook's shank; then bind a thin bunch of Z-lon along the shank, from just behind the hook's eye to its bend.

2. Trim the Z-lon closely, back a little from the eye. Dub a tapered abdomen up half the shank, or just slightly past halfway.

3. Cut a slim strip of buoyant closed-cell foam. Bind the foam atop the hook at the front of the abdomen with *firm* thread-turns (tight turns might cut the foam). Trim the front of the foam closely and bind the end thoroughly.

4. Strip the soft fuzz from the base of a hen-saddle hackle (or use the original starling). The hackle should match, on a hackle gauge, the size of your hook. Bind the hackle by its stem along the shank to the just back from the eye.

5. Trim away the hackle's stem. Advance the thread to just behind the eye. Wind the hackle forward in two to four open spirals over the bare thread-wrappings to the eye. Secure the tip of the hackle under tight thread-turns, just behind the eye. Trim off the hackle's tip.

6. Part the top fibers down the sides or trim them away. Draw the foam forward, and then push it back a little to make it hump up. Secure the foam at the eye with firm thread-turns. Trim the end of the foam, and then build and complete a thread head.

THE DARK CAHILL WET FLY

HOOK:	Heavy wire, standard length to 1X long, sizes 16 to 8.
THREAD:	Black 8/0 or 6/0.
TAIL:	Lemon wood-duck flank (or mallard flank dyed to wood-duck color).
BODY:	Muskrat.
HACKLE:	Brown hen-neck hackle.
WING:	Lemon wood-duck flank (or dyed mallard flank).

(NOTE: for the Light Cahill: cream thread, wood-duck tail, badger underfur or cream-dubbing body, ginger hen hackle, wood-duck wing.)

The Dark Cahill and Light Cahill are a matched set from the Old East school of fly design. Invented by Dan Cahill (though that seems to be in question), these dry-fly patterns were once exceptionally popular on the trout streams of Vermont and New York and Pennsylvania and other places east of the Great Plains. The wet-fly versions of these dry flies are also called the Dark and Light Cahill. Today the wet-fly versions are probably tied and fished about as often as their dry-fly counterparts. This may be due in part to the many new and, theoretically, more imitative dry-fly designs—the no-hackles, parachutes, thorax duns, and others—with which the Cahill dry flies must compete.

But it is also due to a minor resurgence in the use of the traditional wet fly. The wet fly does, after all, look quite a bit like several aquatic insects either in full adulthood or in the final, nearly mature stages of metamorphosis. So a wet Cahill fished not on the traditional lively swing but adrift with only the tiniest added movement—more like struggling than swimming—or even freely adrift, is an imitative fly fully up to current standards.

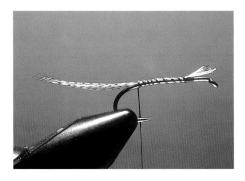

1. Start the thread well up the hook's shank; then bind a small section of wood-duck fibers there. Wind the thread down fibers and shank to the hook's bend, resulting in a tail about half to the full length of the shank.

2. Trim the butts of the fibers closely. Dub a body of fur from the bend to about three quarters up the shank.

Using a hackle gauge, find a hen hackle to match the size of the hook. Strip the base of the hackle's stem.

3. Bind the hackle by its stem at the front of the body; trim the stem closely. Advance the thread just a little ways; then wind the hackle forward in three to five close turns. Bind the tip of the hackle, and then trim it closely.

4. Pinch the hackle down so that its fibers sweep back, but still outward, along the top, bottom, and sides of the body.

Strip the short fibers from the sides of a wood-duck flank feather.

5. Bunch the wood-duck feather, and bind it lightly atop the hook, a little long. Draw the feather slowly forward until it extends just past the rear edge of the bend. Add a few thread-turns, trim the butts of the fibers, and then build and complete a thread head.

SOFT-HACKLED FLIES

A good many fly fishers are probably still uncertain about how a wet fly differs from a soft-hackled fly, and if the differences are even worth bothering with. Wet fly, soft-hackled fly, it's really all the same, isn't it?

No, actually it's not.

Though it *can* be.

Look, here's the simple explanation, or at least half of it. The wet fly is normally fished with the traditional wet-fly swing (and sometimes with a twitching action)—at least a fairly lively retrieve of the fly overall. The soft-hackled fly is fished on a very subtle retrieve with an across- or even slightly *up*stream cast and plenty of line-mending to work the fly ever so slightly. A modest to lively retrieve versus a *very* slow retrieve—see the difference now?

However, I did say that the two fly types can be treated the same, and that's true. The wet fly can be and sometimes is fished in very slow soft-hackle fashion, even, occasionally, dead drift. Still, lively is the norm. The soft-hackled fly? I've never seen one fished quickly. One could be, of course, but its design makes it a poor choice for such work.

All this begs the question that may already have occurred to you: *why* are these two similar fly-styles fished differently?

Good question. And its answer completes the explanation about how wet flies and soft-hackled flies differ.

Answer: the wet fly and soft-hackled fly are fished differently, in part, because they are *designed* to be fished differently.

Wet flies have hackle fibers of standard length, fibers that are supple, yes, but stiff enough not to lie pinned by a good push of water—stiff enough to bounce on an active against-the-current retrieve. The sort of current and retrieve that would put a straitjacket on a soft-hackle fly.

But soft-hackled flies require a different sort of hackle for the quiet retrieves and light currents for which they are intended. Soft-hackled flies have long, supple hackle fibers, the sort that wave like delicate legs when the pressure of water against them is light and varied.

So for soft-hackled flies, you need hackle with especially soft fibers—hen *saddle* (hen neck is okay, but a bit stiff—better for wet flies), partridge flank, starling, and such.

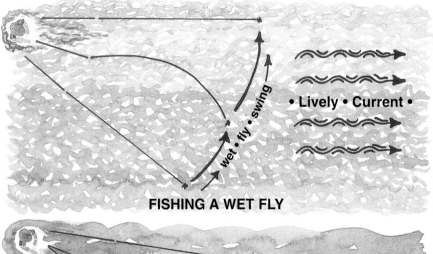

• Lively • Current •

FISHING A WET FLY

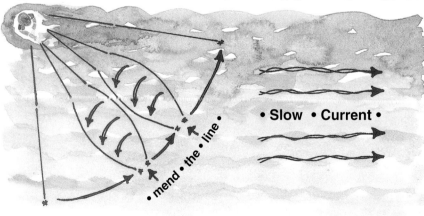

• Slow • Current •

FISHING A SOFT-HACKLED FLY

TYING SOFT-HACKLED FLIES

A body and a hackle—that's all there is to many soft-hackled flies. So when tying such flies you won't often be bothered with adding a lot of common fly components—tail, wings, tag, rib...

Consequently, soft-hackle fly patterns are pretty easy to tie.

Of course, not all soft-hackled fly patterns are the same; if they were, there would be only one. Some do have ribs, some have bodies of floss or herl or dubbing, and so on. Despite all the variations, the two patterns we'll tie—the Partridge and Yellow and the Starling and Herl—are fairly typical soft-hackle fly patterns and should provide a good introduction.

As you'd expect, the hackle of a soft-hackle is the critical element for the tier, and for the effectiveness of the finished fly. Fiber-length is the first order of business. Based on my own experience, and a bit of research, I've concluded that the hackle for a soft-hackle fly should have fibers equal to the full length of the hook, or slightly shorter. A hackle that matches, on a hackle gauge, a hook two sizes larger than the one you're using will be correct.

You can bind the hackle on by its tip, so that when you wrap that hackle its longest fibers will be in front (as I'll demonstrate with the Partridge and Yellow). By wrapping the hackle back to the front of the body and then winding the thread *forward*

through the hackle (as I'll demonstrate with the Starling and Herl), the longest fibers end up in front too; and better yet, turns of thread will cross and reinforce the fragile stem, resulting in a hackle collar that is tough.

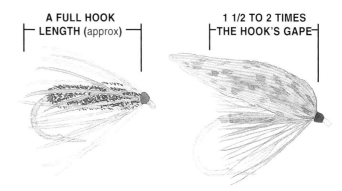

A FULL HOOK LENGTH (approx)

1 1/2 TO 2 TIMES THE HOOK'S GAPE

SOFT-HACKLED FLY   **WET FLY**

HACKLE-FIBER LENGTHS

Carol Ann Morris

PARTRIDGE AND YELLOW

HOOK:	Heavy wire, 1X long, sizes 18 to 10.
THREAD:	Yellow 6/0 or 8/0.
ABDOMEN:	Yellow floss.
THORAX:	Hare's mask fur.
HACKLE:	Gray partridge (or substitute hen saddle hackle).

STARLING AND HERL

HOOK:	Heavy wire, 1X long, sizes 18 to 14.
THREAD:	Black 6/0 or 8/0.
BODY:	Peacock herl.
HACKLE:	Starling body feather with iridescent sheen.

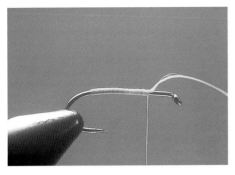

1. Here's how to tie the Partridge and Yellow. Start the thread well up the hook's shank. There, bind on the end of some floss. Wind the thread tightly down floss and shank to the hook's bend, then back up to its starting point. Wind the floss forward in close turns up the shank to the hanging thread. Bind the end of the floss there and trim its end.

2. Spin some hare's mask dubbing onto the thread, and then dub a thick, short thorax over the front third of the shank. (Leave a little bare shank behind the hook's eye, for the hackle and thread head.)

3. Find a gray partridge feather of appropriate size for your hook. (For more on hackle-fiber length for soft-hackled flies, see "Tying Soft-Hackled Flies" on the previous page.) Stroke the fibers back from the tip of the feather, and then bind the feather at the front of the thorax by that tip. Wind the thread forward to just behind the eye.

4. Trim away the tip of the feather. Wind the feather forward in two to four close turns (depending on how full you want the hackle). Bind the butt of the feather with a few tight thread-turns just behind the eye. Trim off the stem.

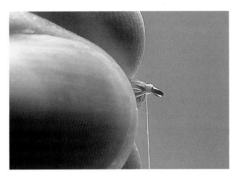

5. Stroke all the partridge fibers back from the eye. build a tapered thread-head, whip finish and trim the thread, and then add head cement to the thread-head to complete the Partridge and Yellow.

Carol Ann Morris

1. Here's how to tie the Starling and Herl. Start the thread at about the center of the shank; then spiral the thread back to the bend. At the bend, bind on a few peacock herls. Spin the herls and working thread together to form a sort of herl-rope. Wind this rope up the shank to just short of the eye. There, unwind the herl from the thread and bind the herl with a few tight thread-turns. Trim the ends of the herl closely.

2. Here's another way to wrap a hackle on a soft-hackled fly. Find a starling feather of appropriate size (as described on the previously page under "Tying Soft-Hackled Flies."). Strip the fibers from the base of the feather. Bind the feather right behind the hook's eye; then wind the thread *back* to the front of the body. Trim off the feather's stem.

3. Wind the hackle in two to four close turns *back* to the front of the body; then spiral the thread *forward* through the hackle to the eye. Find and then trim out the feather's tip. Build and complete a thread head as described previously for the Partridge and Yellow to complete the Starling and Herl.

THE PARTRIDGE CADDIS EMERGER

HOOK:	Standard dry-fly hook, sizes 20 to 12.
THREAD:	Olive 8/0.
SHUCK:	Fine kinky olive Z-lon for larger hooks, Antron yarn for smaller.
RIB:	Fine copper wire.
ABDOMEN:	Olive Antron dubbing.
WING:	Two brown partridge feathers over a little olive Z-lon (Antron for small hooks).
THORAX:	Arizona Peacock Dubbing (originally, peacock herl).
COMMENTS:	Above is the olive version. The tan version includes tan thread, abdomen, shuck, and under-wing with Arizona Bronze Peacock Dubbing for the thorax.

Idaho's Henrys Fork of the Snake River is widely acknowledged as one tough place to catch a trout. Slow clear water; an abundance of insect feed; and an abundance of pestiferous fly fishermen roaming the banks with lofty intentions of hooking, playing, and releasing their catch make the rainbow trout of Henrys Fork downright fastidious. Ideal fish, really, for fly testing, and the very fish that helped Mike Lawson develop his Partridge Caddis Emerger.

Designed for the Fork and proved just as effective on such other quiet streams as the Big Hole and upper Missouri, the Partridge Caddis Emerger is a fly for caddis hatches in slow currents. Mike usually fishes it up halfway in the air, half down in the water (a little floatant on only the wing does it), like a partly hatched caddisfly that's in trouble and isn't going to complete its transition—a "cripple," anglers call it. Being incapable of flying away, it is especially attractive to trout. (He also fishes his Partridge Caddis Emerger entirely sunk, a few inches down, suspended below a high-floating dry fly.)

Sure, you can fish dry flies or pupa-imitating nymphs during caddis hatches—plenty of fly fishers do. But if your trout are "fastidious," consider the Partridge Caddis Emerger.

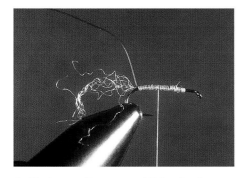

1. Bind a small amount of Z-lon (or Antron, for smaller hooks), and then copper wire, back along the hook's shank to the its bend. Trim the forward ends of the Z-lon and wire closely.

2. Dub a full abdomen up about two thirds to three quarters of the shank. Wind the copper wire up the abdomen in five or six ribs. Bind the end of the wire with a few tight thread-turns, and then trim it.

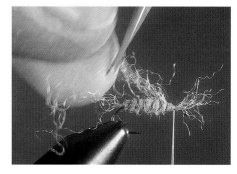

3. Bind a small amount of Z-lon (or Antron, if you used Antron for the shuck) atop the shank right in front of the abdomen. Trim the Z-lon directly over the far edge of the bend. Trim the front of the Z-lon closely.

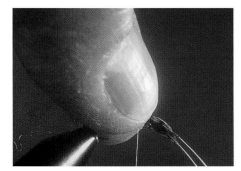

4. Set two partridge feathers (their bases stripped of fluff) one atop the other, tips evened. Bind the feathers, with cupped sides down, atop the hook right in front of the abdomen.

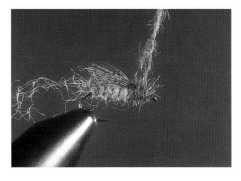

5. Note that the tips of the feathers terminate directly over the rear of the abdomen.
Trim off the feathers' butts. Dub a full, somewhat rough thorax.

6. Build a small tapered thread head; whip finish and then trim the thread. Trim the shuck to equal the full length of the shank. Add head cement to the thread head.

Grouped Dry Flies, Nymphs, Emergers, and such

The outsize pupa of the October Caddis.

Stalking nervous trout on a tiny spring creek.

Spying on trout.

TYING TINY FOR FALL TROUT

The western March browns and PMDs—modest-size mayflies—and the *Rhyocophilla* and *Hydropsyche* caddisflies are busy closing up shop for the winter by late September. In the coastal states, the hulking October Caddis begins to show around Labor Day and continues hatching through October. There may also be the odd minuscule caddisflies and beetles around, but when the swelter of summer dissolves into crisp fall air the heaviest and most dependable hatches on most streams will be tiny *Baetis* and even tinier *Tricorythodes* mayflies. Second to the mayflies will be the midges, which seem to live everywhere there is water and, in moving water at least, can be positively diminutive.

Imitating tiny insects requires tiny flies. So for the fly tier, fall is a chance to revive skills and revisit strategies for tying on hooks of size 18 and smaller. The skills, I'll leave you to practice. The strategies, we'll examine shortly.

One theory regarding tiny-fly design, and I support it, is this: When an insect, and therefore its imitation, is really small, trout have trouble inspecting it for detail; consequently, they concentrate less on detail with tiny insects, and their imitations, than they do on insects of greater size. In other words, flies tied on a hook of size 18 or smaller are best kept plain.

This is good news for the fly tier. It means that the challenge of tying on little hooks is diminished by the austere designs of the flies he'll tie on them.

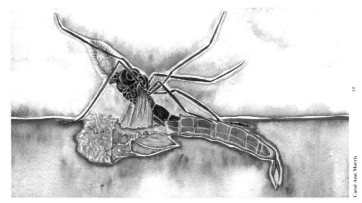

A hatching midge.

slowly on the water after releasing her eggs—she is what fly fishers call a "spinner." A soft-hackle fly, in its simplest form for tiny hooks, is just a dubbed body and some sort of supple hackle; it is fished barely submerged and with only the slightest movement to suggest an insect struggling to escape its shuck and the water's dense surface; it can function as a hatching mayfly or caddisfly. The Brassie can be tied from tiny to substantial, but is nothing more than a copper-wire body and a dubbed thorax, a simple and effective nymph often tied tiny to imitate a midge larva, sometimes a caddis larva, and even a mayfly nymph. These are a few of the tiny fly-patterns I commonly tie and fish. There are many other good ones, but these six make an excellent starting selection.

A freshly hatched mayfly "dun," the immature adult of the genus Baetis.

What, then, are these simple fly patterns for tiny hooks? The Griffith's Gnat is surely one, just a hackle spiraled over a herl body—that's all! It imitates a midge hatching at the surface. The Sparkle Dun imitates a mayfly dun not quite fully hatched, and consists of only a yarn-tuft shuck, a fanned-hair wing, and a body. The Black Ant (and its complement, the Cinnamon Ant) is just some fine dubbing built up in two ant-like swellings with the slender thread-layered shank between spiraled with a bit of hackle. The Poly-Wing Spinner imitates the female mayfly adult, dying

Fly-fishing guide Tom Baltz displays some of the miniscule flies he trusts on Pennsylvania's Letort Spring Run.

GRIFFITH'S GNAT
George Griffith

HOOK: Standard dry fly or short shank, sizes 24 (or even smaller) to 16.
THREAD: Olive or black 8/0.
HACKLE: Grizzly.
BODY: Peacock herl.

SPARKLE DUN
Craig Mathews & John Juracek

HOOK: Dry fly or short, sizes 22 to 16.
THREAD: Body-color 8/0.
WING: Coastal deer hair.
SHUCK: Brown Antron or Z-lon yarn.
BODY: Fine synthetic dubbing.

BLACK ANT & CINNAMON ANT

HOOK: Dry fly or short, sizes 20 to 16.
THREAD: Black (or brown) 8/0.
HUMPS: Black (or cinnamon) synthetic dubbing.
HACKLE: Black (or brown), one.

POLY WING SPINNER

HOOK: Dry fly or short, sizes 24 to 16.
THREAD: Body-color 8/0.
TAIL: Hackle fibers, split.
BODY: Fine synthetic dubbing.
WING: Gray or white Poly yarn.

BAETIS SOFT HACKLE
Rick Hafele

HOOK: Heavy wire, 1X long, sizes 20 to 14.
THREAD: Gray 6/0 or 8/0.
TAIL: Blue-dun hackle fibers.
BODY: Gray dubbing.
HACKLE: Blue-dun hen hackle.

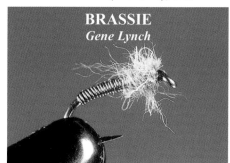

BRASSIE
Gene Lynch

HOOK: Heavy wire, 1X or 2X long, sizes 20 to 16.
THREAD: Black 8/0.
ABDOMEN: Fine copper wire.
THORAX: Muskrat fur.

TYING STRATEGIES FOR TINY FLIES

TOOLS: For the most part, forget special tools—the same hackle pliers, scissors, bobbin, and other tools you use for tying on a size-10 hook will probably work perfectly well with a size-22. The exception may be your vise—if it's jaws are too thick, they'll make tying a Griffith's Gnat a clumsy effort, one that could have been comfortably managed with slimmer jaws. There are vises made just for tying tiny, but a less expensive solution than buying a second vise is to select a more versatile vise in the first place, one with jaws slim enough to serve efficiently through a large range of hook sizes. Another solution is to buy a vise that takes alternate jaws for extra-small or extra-large hooks. But if you already have a vise that's poor with little hooks, then consider buying a "midge head," a small tiny-fly vise-head that locks into the jaws of a conventional vise.

MATERIALS: Fine, thin, small, whatever—the point is, materials for tiny flies should provide little bulk and proper proportions in the completed fly. This can mean choosing materials with care—very fine, very soft dubbing rather than heavy and coarse; fine gold wire instead of oval gold tinsel, for example—or applying materials with care—using only wisps of dubbing for a body or a narrow section of turkey quill in a wing case for a minimum of bulk. Or it can mean both. Thread is a big factor in tying tiny flies. There are now some very fine threads that handle well and are quite strong. Use them if you wish; I use 8/0 thread for almost all my flies on hooks from size-18 to -24—and, for that matter, often up to size-8. The trick is to use no more turns of thread than required to properly do the job; in other words: if five turns of thread are enough to firmly secure a hackle tip, do not use seven.

MAGNIFICATION: Now in my fifties, I can't imagine tying a size-20 soft-hackled fly without my binocular magnifier. It's a pair of lenses formed in a single plate, mounted in a visor which, in turn, is mounted on an adjustable head band. But reading glasses can do the same work, as can the variety of magnifiers made specifically for tying flies. The point is, tying on minute hooks is for most tiers much easier with magnification than without it. If you don't know what power of magnification you need, try around 2.75X.

On the left, a vise head whose jaws hold solidly a size-2 hook, yet are narrow enough for comfortable tying on the size 20 they contain. On the right, a midge head.

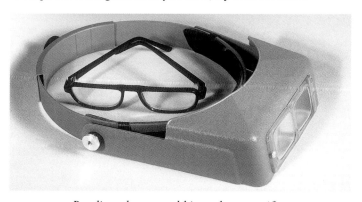

Reading glasses and binocular magnifier.

TYING A *BAETIS* SOFT HACKLE

1. Start the thread on the hook's shank. Strip about half-a-dozen fibers from one side of a hen-neck hackle. Bind the fibers along the shank; the length of the fibers, from where they project from the hook's bend, should be two thirds to the full length of the shank.

2. Trim the butts of the hackle fibers closely. Dub a slim, slightly tapered body up the shank to just back from the hook's eye.

The wisp of dubbing on the upper right is about all you'd use for the entire body on this tiny hook. Honest!

3. Select a hen hackle of the proper size for your hook using a hackle gauge. Strip the longer fibers from the base of the hackle's stem. (For a really sparse hackle, strip one side of the stem entirely.) Bind the hackle to the shank at the front of the body. Trim the hackle's stem closely.

4. With the thread hanging close to the eye, wind the hackle forward in two turns—the fibers should appear sparse. Bind the tip of the hackle; then trim the tip closely. Build a small tapered thread head, whip finish the thread and trim it, add head cement to the thread head.

TYING A TINY SPARKLE DUN

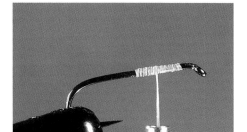

1. Start the thread just behind the hook's eye, wrap it back to the middle of the hook's shank, then forward halfway up the first layer of thread.

2. Stack a small bunch of deer hair for the wing—a small bunch. In so small a fly, the stacking must be good, so stack carefully, and handle the hair deliberately.

Bind the hair atop the shank, at the point where the thread was hanging.

Trim the butts of the hair to a taper; then bind them with tight thread-turns.

3. Proportions are especially important on tiny flies—the wing's length should equal the distance from the hook's eye to the middle of its bend. Measure carefully. I often use my scissors as a measuring tool, as in the previous photograph.

Bind on yarn for a shuck (very little); then trim off its forward end. Dub a slender body to the rear of the wing.

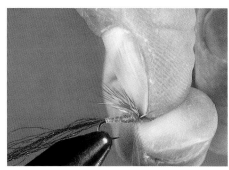

4. Push your thumbnail back under the hair and atop the hook; then push back firmly as you tip the nail up, as in the photograph, to crease the hair upright. You can repeat this process on the sides of the hair, if necessary. Stroke the hair back firmly; then hold it there as you build plenty of tight turns of bare (not dubbed) thread. This will lock the wing upright, in a half-fan shape.

5. Dub around the wing, crisscrossing the dubbed thread forward and back beneath the wing. Build a little dubbing in front of the wing. (Remember—keep the dubbing thin.) Build a small tapered thread head, whip finish the thread, trim the thread closely, and then add head cement to the head. Trim the yarn-shuck; it should extend out one half to the full length of the hook.

KAMLOOPS STILLWATER STANDARDS

Though Canada and the United States share a border spanning more than 3,000 miles, and though several major Canadian cities lie so close to that border that a leisurely afternoon drive can carry their inhabitants across it to mingle with their American neighbors, and though Canada covers even more square miles than does the US, most Americans know as much about this vast country as they know about the sport of curling. And so it is with American fly fishers—they know almost nothing about Canadian fishing and flies.

But Canada is blessed with an abundance of fine fishing and an abundance of inventive fly tiers. Both are worth knowing.

In western Canada a lot of that fine fishing involves trout lakes, largely because of the Kamloops Lake Region in the province of British Columbia. Fly fishers there will tell you that within an hour's drive of the little town of Kamloops lie over 220 trout lakes. And they are rich lakes indeed—my friend Brian Chan, the fisheries biologist there, says that a three-inch trout put into a good Kamloops lake in May should be two-pounder by November.

As you'd expect, this kind of fishing attracts a lot of dedicated anglers and inspires a lot of theories (said theories requiring long hours of testing in the field—such sacrifice!). The flies that have resulted from all this deserve consideration on both sides of that vast aforementioned border.

Brian Chan, for over two decades the senior fisheries biologist for the Kamloops lakes. An eminent lake fisher, Brian collaborated with Skip on the book Morris & Chan on Fly Fishing Trout Lakes.

A Kamloops rainbow trout.

A typical lake in the Kamloops region of British Columbia, Canada.

58   MORRIS ON TYING FLIES

THE CANADIAN CHRONICLES

It's easy enough to figure out which flies are currently popular in western Canada (especially if you've spent as much time there as I have in the past few years). And, mostly, it isn't that hard to determine which of those flies have been around for a while—mess about long enough with fly patterns and you'll learn to approximate one's age by its materials and design (and often be pretty accurate).

But the going can get tough when you begin digging around for histories. Many flies just appear and become popular, and all that anyone is certain of are their names (and sometimes no one's even sure about that).

Books don't forget or become confused (to be confused, a book must be so upon publication; it cannot later acquire that quality), so I sought out some helpful ones. The first I found was *'The Gillie,'* published in 1985, with those curious single quotation marks surrounding its title. It's a compilation book with a dozen authors, each contributing one or more of its twenty-one chapters. The authors all struck me as seasoned and knowledgeable.

Then I found *Fly Patterns of British Columbia*, by Arthur Lingren. Published in 1996, it seems well-researched and discusses the histories of all but two of the fly patterns that follow.

Although I did find a few more books that mentioned western Canadian flies, they added nothing important to the information of the previous two.

Finally, I relied on friends from the Kamloops Region: fly fisher-fisheries biologist Brian Chan and fly-fishing guide Gordon Honey.

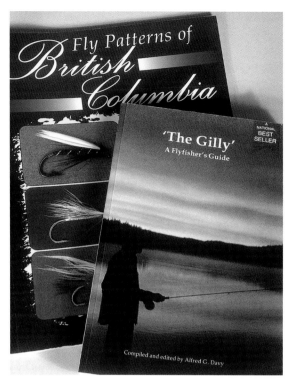

The books Skip used as reference for this article.

THE TEST

The flies we'll explore are very popular among Canadian lake fishers, and have been around for at least (I'm nearly certain) two decades. They all share one quality in particular that accounts for their inclusion in this article: They have passed the longevity test, having remained popular for many years and right up to the present.

Among them are some surprises. (Canadian fly fishers will be especially surprised at the omission of the Halfback nymph. Fear not—the Halfback has its very own article-chapter on page 32.)

We begin with the nymphs, the staples of trout-lake fishing, but more radical are the dry flies that follow them.

Carol Ann Morris

CAREY SPECIAL

The Carey Special, according to Lingren, was created by a retired British officer named Colonel Carey, some time during the 1920s, making it the oldest of the patterns here. Lingren says the original dressing probably consisted largely of ground-hog fur. It may also have had a rib of black linen thread.

But I met a very different Carey Special when I took up lake fishing, as a boy, around Seattle, Washington in the early 1960s. It was a wildly popular fly then, with a tail and hackle of pheasant rump (which was consequently available in sporting goods stores and our one or two fly shops) and a body usually of peacock herl or chenille. I'll go ahead with the version of the Carey I know, simply *because* I know it. Actually, I more than just know it; it seems now like an old friend.

What, exactly, the Carey imitates—or if it imitates anything at all—has long been in contention. Lingren quotes the eminent Canadian writer Roderick Haig-Brown from his book

The Western Angler:

> Whether or not it was originally tied as an imitation of some natural insect I do not know, but it has an extremely lifelike action in the water and may well be taken for a dragon-fly nymph.

Lingren also quotes Steve Raymond, from his book *Kamloops*, who describes the Carey as representing the caddis pupa. In any case, Haig-Brown sums up the whole business elsewhere in Lingren's quote when he says the Carey Special,

> besides being one of the best killers, is as somberly dressed as any natural...

In other words, who cares what trout take it for?—it works.

CAREY SPECIAL	Colonel Carey
HOOK:	Heavy wire, 1X to 4X long, sizes 10 to 4.
THREAD:	Black 8/0, 6/0, or 3/0.
TAIL:	Pheasant rump (or badger hair).
BODY:	Peacock herl, or black or dark-olive chenille.
HACKLE:	Pheasant rump.

DOC SPRATLEY

'*The Gilly*' describes the Doc Spratley, which was created in the early 1940s, as a "famous trolling fly" of British Columbia, and adds that in varied sizes it can be used to imitate "most of the major insects as well as leeches." Although the Doc Spratley has a bit of a reputation as an old timer's fly, it still rides out a lot of casts and accounts for a lot of trout all over western Canada.

Overall, the Doc Spratley is fairly traditional, and a fairly easy fly to tie. The only possible problem for most tiers will be forming a herl head over the tapered bindings of the wing and throat—herl is slippery, and likes to slide down such inclines. Certainly, dubbing could replace the herl. But if you do use herl, I suggest you spin it around the working thread, for durability.

DOC SPRATLEY	Dick Prankard
HOOK:	Heavy wire, 1X to 3X long, sizes 12 to 6.
THREAD:	Black 8/0 or 6/0.
TAIL:	Guinea flank-feather fibers.
RIB:	Flat silver tinsel (there seems to be no standard width).
BODY:	Black wool yarn.
WING:	Pheasant-tail or -rump fibers.
THROAT:	Guinea flank-feather fibers.
HEAD:	Peacock herl.

TUNKWANAMID

'*The Gilly*' describes this fly as among the "original chironomid patterns of B.C." (British Columbia), and Lingren says that it was developed by a man named Tom Murray during the early 1970s. Considering how immensely popular the fishing of an imitation chironomid pupa now is in western Canada, I find it surprising that the whole business was nearly unknown even three decades ago.

Certainly no lake fisher should be without imitations of the chironomid (which stream fishers call a "midge"); it is the most ubiquitous of the lake insects upon which trout feed, not only in Canada but almost anywhere in North America. And the Tunkwanamid is a proven imitation.

There's no mystery regarding which Kamloops lake accounts for the name Tunkwanamid. (Here's a hint, it's one of the following: Leighton, Roche, Tunkwa, Lac Le Jeune.)

Don't let the bright-silver rib convince you that this really isn't an imitative fly—because it is. Anyone who has seen a chironomid pupa ripe to hatch will understand—the body is encased in a bloated husk, shining like silver from its clear, reflective composition and from the gasses it contains. The only advice anyone might need for tying this fly is this: Before winding the herl, twist it with the thread. The herl becomes much tougher that way. (Although the rib probably protects the fragile herl fairly well.)

The popular long-leader-and-floating-line approach for fishing a chironomid is a common approach with the Tunkwanamid. Following the cast is a ridiculously long pause to let the fly sink, then an even more ridiculously slow retrieve.

TUNKWANAMID *Tom Murray*

HOOK:	Heavy wire, 1X or 2X long, sizes 16 to 8.
THREAD:	Black 8/0 or 6/0.
TAG:	Fine oval silver tinsel.
RIB:	The same tinsel used for the tag, continuing up the body.
BODY:	Peacock herl.
GILLS:	White ostrich herl.

DRY FLIES

On the Kamloops lakes, fly fishers are almost as likely to throw dry flies at rising trout as to draw leech imitations slowly and deeply over shoals, which is not typical lake fishing, in my experience. But the nature of these Canadian lakes *isn't* typical—most have few edible small fishes to distract the trout from their abundance of insects. When those insects rise to hatch, to burst from shucks and unfurl wings, up come the trout and out come the dry flies. Other times, when there is no hatch, dry flies work perhaps because the trout are just used to finding food on top.

The two dry flies to come—the Tom Thumb and Mikulak Sedge—suggest an evolution of fly tying that is fairly free of American trends just across the border. US tiers will find these flies intriguing and fresh, as will uninitiated Canadian tiers and anyone unfamiliar with them. (The Tom Thumb and its pattern, history, and use were originally included in this article. But since that fly has its own article elsewhere in this book where it is examined in depth and tied by steps, I've omitted it here.)

MIKULAK SEDGE

Here is a twist new to most fly tiers (most *American* fly tiers, anyway)—a hair wing built in two or three bunches up the body and incorporating the bunch normally considered a tail. It's a buoyant fly, for imitating adult caddisflies skittering across a lake's surface, as they often do immediately upon hatching. (Canadians and British often refer to caddisflies as "sedges," hence the name of this fly.)

But for all its popularity, the Mikulak Sedge is mysteriously absent from *'The Gilly'* and Lingren's book. Nevertheless, it is a standard on Canadian lakes, especially when the enormous traveling sedge begins its spring-summer hatching, bringing big trout to slash at the surface and dedicated travelling-sedge followers to cast Mikulak Sedges amid the action.

According to a friend of Art Mikulak's, Gordon Honey tells me, Mikulak developed his fly in the early 1970s and christened it on Roche Lake in the Kamloops area.

Gordon is a real fan of the Mikulak Sedge and says that he has been fishing it in various sizes and colors "exclusively for caddis over the last three years." Remember, I am speaking here of a full-time fly-fishing guide, a man who fishes at least 100 days a year on lakes with fine hatches of caddisflies. A fly could have no better recommendation than that.

It is logical to conclude from all this that American fly fishers are missing a world of often bright, sometimes quirky, fresh innovation if they ignore Canadian fly fishing and fly tying. Sound conclusion.

MIKULAK SEDGE

HOOK:	Light wire, 2X long, sizes 12 to 6.
THREAD:	Eight-ought or 6/0 to match the body's color.
TAIL (wing):	Naturally light elk hair. (That's for the traveling sedge; for imitating other caddis use either light or dark elk.)
BODY:	Green synthetic dubbing. (That's for the traveling sedge; for imitating other caddis use tan, brown, gray—whatever's appropriate.)
WING:	Same as the tail, added in two or three bunches up the body.
HEAD:	The butts of the last wing-hair-bunch, trimmed blunt.
HACKLE:	One, brown.

TYING THE CAREY SPECIAL

1. Start the thread well up the hook's shank, and then bind a bunch of pheasant-rump fibers atop the shank for a tail. The tail should be about as long as the hook's gape is wide.

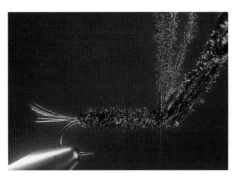

2. Bind several peacock herls (about twelve for a size-8 hook, for example) to the shank by the hook's bend. Twist the herls around the thread and then wind the resulting herl-rope up the shank to just back from the hook's eye.

3. Separate the herls from the thread and bind, then trim off, their ends.

Strip the fluff from the base of a pheasant-rump feather. Bind the feather by its bare stem with tight thread-turns just behind the eye. Notice that some of the the feather's fiber-tips are broken—typical of pheasant-rump, but no problem on a Carey Special.

4. Trim off the stem of the feather. Using hackle pliers, wind the feather forward in two to four turns. Secure the feather's tip under a few tight thread-turns; then trim off the tip.

Stroke back the fibers and hold them there as you build up a tapered thread head. Whip finish the thread, trim it, and then add head cement to the thread head.

TYING THE TUNKWANAMID

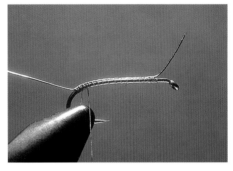

1. Start the thread about 1/16 of an inch back from the hook's eye. There, bind the end of some oval tinsel. Spiral the thread tightly down the tinsel and the hook's shank to slightly down the hook's bend. Wind the thread back up the bend a few turns. Closely trim the end of the tinsel, if necessary.

2. Bind several peacock herls (at least four) to the shank just slightly ahead of the rearmost thread-turns. Spin the herls and the thread together into a sort of herl-rope, then wind that rope up the shank to near, but just a bit short of, the eye.

3. Unravel the end of the herl from the thread and then bind the herl and trim its ends closely. Wind the tinsel forward in a few close turns to form a tag behind the herl; then continue winding the tinsel, now in open spirals, "ribs," over the herl-body. At the front of the body, bind the end of the tinsel and then trim it.

4. At the rear of the short space remaining between the body and the hook's eye, bind a single ostrich herl. Spin the herl with the thread and wind the resulting fluffy rope forward in close turns. Unravel the herl from the thread; then bind the end of the herl, trim it closely, build and complete the usual thread head.

THREE FLIES FOR THE GREAT WESTERN CADDIS

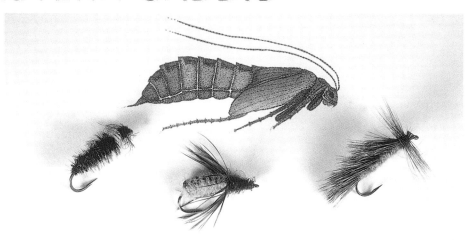

Skip's favorite flies for imitating the three stages of the October Caddis, scattered across a Carol Ann Morris painting of the pupa.

Among my western fishing friends, the ones who know their stuff, I've observed a trend: They now believe it is the *pupa* of the massive October Caddis—not the adult—to which trout give their greatest attention. Most fly fishers focus on the adult because it's enormous and showy. Try to ignore it and one may bat you in the face on its erratic flight. However, caddisflies fluttering wildly up in the air don't make much of an impression on trout holding down in river currents.

But be warned: Imitating all *three* stages of the October Caddis *can* be productive, and you'd be wise to prepare yourself with a fly for each stage. That's what I do now, after a couple of decades of chasing the hatch. And I have culled my way through many fly patterns over the years until I now carry mostly just

these three: the Deschutes Cased Caddis, Brick Back Caddis, and Mikulak Sedge.

What you need to know about the October Caddis in general is that of its five species, you'll find the largest representatives and heaviest populations in the Pacific Northwest—the great caddis is abundant in such rivers as Washington State's Yakima and Oregon's Deschutes—and that other western states generally have smaller insects in smaller numbers, though sufficient numbers for good fishing and to require imitative flies. You also need to know that this caddis lives strictly in currents—you'll never find one in a lake or a pond. (Though there are stillwater caddisflies of similar *appearance* and of good size that might make you think otherwise).

Carol Ann Morris

A Deschutes River rainbow displaying the Brick Back Caddis for which it fell.

LARVA

Throughout most of its life, the October Caddis creeps about the slower parts of rivers as a larva, dragging its abdomen behind it in a heavy shell (fly fishers call it a "case") it builds from sand and tiny pebbles. Trout occasionally get a shot at a naked pupa that's outgrown its case and was building the next when the current caught it, but that's rare. Normally, trout just eat the works, then process out the good stuff and eliminate the case as a little sand.

I've fished John Hazel's Deschutes Cased Caddis successfully, especially on the Deschutes River, for years. It's been effective from spring through summer, though I go to imitating the pupa just as soon as the hatch begins, so I can't say how John's fly would fare after that. But since the larva live for up to three years, this fly could conceivably be effective throughout every season. The Deschutes

Cased Caddis isn't always the best choice, for the Deschutes or anywhere else, but sometimes trout do seem in a mood for shooting down a corpulent caddis, regardless of the gravel chaser.

The Deschutes Cased Caddis is easy enough to tie, and its convincing peacock-and-hackle simulated case has always impressed me as a clever solution to a familiar fly-tier's puzzle. It's a durable and effective design.

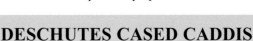

Fish the Deschutes Cased Caddis dead-drift, right along the bottom with the standard dry-line-and-indicator technique for nymphs in rivers.

Carol Ann Morris

DESCHUTES CASED CADDIS
John Hazel

HOOK:	Heavy wire, 2X to 4X long, size 10 to 6.
THREAD:	Black 3/0.
WEIGHT:	Lead or lead-substitute wire.
RIB:	Fine copper wire.
ABDOMEN:	Peacock herls and one brown rooster hackle.
THORAX:	White rabbit dubbing.
HEAD:	Black goat fur (or substitute black hare's mask or squirrel body.)

TYING NOTES: Lead wraps cover the rear two thirds of the hook's shank, and are tapered with dubbing at the rear end. The hackle is bound at the front of the herl-abdomen, then the front third of the shank is dubbed most of the way to the hook's eye. The hackle is then spiraled back to the bend in open spirals, and the wire is spiraled forward through the hackle, and then up the dubbed thorax as three or four ribs. Then the head is dubbed and picked out and the hackle is trimmed short.

PUPA

My days of concentrating on big dry flies for the October Caddis hatch are past—it's the pupal stage on which I now primarily focus. And so, I'm convinced, do trout. During my last float trip down the Deschutes River, for example, I hooked trout all day long on my Brick Back Caddis—an imitation of the October Caddis pupa—and landed a steelhead to boot. Two were my biggest Deschutes trout ever. That evening the adult caddis began their nervous flights. I put up a Mikulak Sedge and began twitching and pausing it along the riverbank and out as far as I thought a fluttering adult might go. Half an hour later I'd landed two lively twelve-inch rainbows. They were fun, but do the math. Pupal imitation—lots of trout, some big ones among them (and a steelhead!), with steady action throughout the day. Adult imitation—two twelve-inchers (though...they *were* lively). Anyway, *that's* why I concentrate on the pupa.

It took me two years of tinkering to come up with the Brick Back, but I knew what I wanted all along—the sparkle of the natural's bubble-crusted, gas-swollen shuck; the stair-step pattern of brown bars running up its back; all in a fast-sinking imitation with an abdomen convincingly crooked and bulged—and I finally got

it. So I showed the final variation of my pattern to trout, and they quickly approved it.

You can cast the Brick Back Caddis upstream to let it sink as it drifts past, then swing it slowly up and in towards the bank at the end, which is probably pretty close to what the natural does—caddis pupa are typically strong swimmers. But I seldom do all that. First, it's not always easy to find a place I can manage this sink-and-swing retrieve on many of the streams I fish. Second, the strike indicator that is so helpful through the drift turns awkward and unnatural on the swing. And third, fishing the Brick Back dead drift below an indicator has been so productive for me that I feel no need to fish the fly otherwise. A free-drifting pupa makes sense anyway—my entomologist friend Rick Hafele tells me that a fair number of defective pupa escape their cases only to struggle weakly as they're swept along the riverbed. Consider: if *you* were a trout, would you rather chase athletic pupae across the currents, or just let the cripples drift up to your nose? I can't imagine anyone preferring the first option, but if you do, then at least you now know what sort of trout you'd be (tired, often hungry, and considered a little dim by the other trout).

BRICK BACK CADDIS (October Caddis) *Skip Morris*

HOOK: Heavy wire, long shank (I prefer a hook with a sort of French curve, like the hook in the photos, the Daiichi 1260), sizes 10 to 6.

BEAD: Black metal, 1/8-inch.

WEIGHT: Lead or lead-substitute wire, one layer of 0.015-inch over a layer of 0.020-inch.

THREAD: Brown 3/0. (You can switch to brown 8/0 or 6/0 after the abdomen is formed, if you prefer.)

ABDOMEN: Amber and orange rabbit fur mixed with fine, chopped silver, pearl, and yellow Mylar strands, like Angel Hair or Lite Brite (or just buy Arizona Flyfishing's Sparkle Nymph Dubbing in the color "Skip's October Caddis"). The bars are made with brown Poly yarn. (Substitutes for the Poly yarn include Stretch Flex or Scud Back, Antron yarn, and—if you want a truly *brilliant* fly—Krystal Flash or Flashabou.)

LEGS: One grizzly-dyed-brown or brown hen saddle or hen-neck hackle. (My favorite is Whiting's "Soft Hackle.")

EYES: Extra-small black pre-made plastic barbell eyes. (Eyes are optional without a bead, but always omit them if you use a bead.)

THORAX: Dark-brown rabbit mixed with fine, chopped silver, pearl, and brown Mylar, or just dark-brown rabbit (or Arizona Flyfishing's Sparkle Nymph Dubbing in "Dark Brown").

Carol Ann Morris

ADULT

While I do believe the adult October Caddis and its imitations have been overrated in the past, I also believe the dry fly has its place with this hatch. Once the hatch is well under way, female adults herald the event by fluttering all about a stream's edges, dropping briefly to the water now and then to release their eggs. This activity reaches its peak near dark, when trout may station themselves all along the banks in wait for a plump caddis. The fly fisher can hope for real action then by if he, or she, drifts and twitches a big caddis-like dry fly from in close to about as far out as the insects are flying.

Experience has lead me to prefer the Mikulak Sedge for this

Carol Ann Morris

work, a fly that's been a hit in Canada for years. Its wing, built in short sections, is highly buoyant and holds its form much better than typical long-wing dry flies. Some build the wing with deer hair, but I find elk more buoyant and slower to absorb water and consequently always use it.

MIKULAK SEDGE (October Caddis version)
Art Mikulak

HOOK: Light wire, 2X long, sizes 8 and 6.

THREAD: Orange 8/0 or 6/0.

TAIL (part of wing): Natural light-brown elk hair.

WING and BODY: Sections of natural light-brown elk hair and yellow-orange synthetic dubbing (Antron, Superfine Dry Fly Dubbing, Poly Dubbing...).

HACKLE: One, brown.

HEAD: The butts of the final bunch of elk hair, cut straight across, over the eye.

TYING NOTES: Comb and stack a small bunch of elk, and then bind it on the hook's shank as a gape-long tail (which is actually the rear of the wing). Dub a little up the shank. Trim the butts of the elk. Bind on another section of elk hair, dub ahead, trim the butts, another section of elk, dub...until you've created three or four wing sections (not including the wing-tail). Leave enough room behind the hook's eye for a head and several turns of hackle. Cut the butts of the last bunch as a short stub—this represents the head.

TYING THE BRICK BACK CADDIS

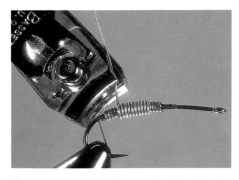

1. Wind a layer of 0.020-inch lead wire over the rear half of the hook's shank. Start the thread on the shank and then bind the lead. Wind a short layer of 0.015-inch lead wire over the center of the first layer of lead, and then bind it.

(If you want a fly with a bead, slip the bead, the small end of its hole forward, up to the hook's eye before winding on the lead.)

2. Wax the thread and then spin dubbing onto it. Dub a ball right against the rear end of the lead—make the ball thick.

(To make the dubbing, simply follow the instructions for making the dubbing in "The Raccoon," on page 100. Or just use Arizona Flyfishing's Sparkle Nymph Dubbing in the color "Skip's October Caddis.")

3. Bind the square-cut end of a length of poly yarn in the center of the lead windings. Bind the yarn back to, even a little way onto, the ball of dubbing. The lead and the end of the yarn will create a bulge near the center the completed abdomen—like the bulge in the abdomen of a real October caddis pupa.

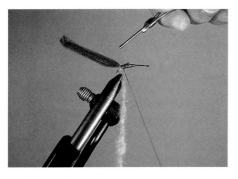

4. Dub fairly generously along several inches of the thread (at least eight inches for a size-8 hook, for example). Draw more thread off your bobbin, a few inches more than the length covered in dubbing. Double the thread back to the hook, and then wrap back over its end a little ways, creating a dubbing loop.

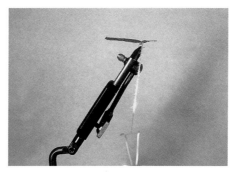

5. Wind the thread up to the hook's eye, whip finish it, and cut it. With a dubbing whirl or dubbing twister, spin the thread loop to gather up and lock in all the dubbing.

6. Clamp a pair of English hackle pliers to the end of the loop. Make three or four turns of the dubbing loop directly in front of the yarn.

You can clutch the pliers in your palm or hang them by their loop from a finger, and hold any part of the dubbing loop you like as you wind it on.

7. Pull the yarn forward and down, and then secure it with one tight turn of the dubbing loop. The result should be a little bar of brown yarn over the dubbing.

8. Continue dubbing and making little bars over layers of dubbing, each bar separated from the last by a turn of the dubbing-loop. After the first bar, you can just hold the yarn in your left hand and the dubbing loop in your right (for right-handers, that is) throughout the rest of the operation; all that's required is a little experimentation and reaching. (Though it's no big deal if you choose to switch hands as often as you like.)

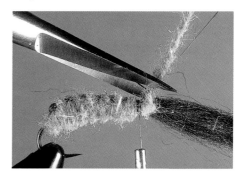

9. Once you've covered about two thirds (to three quarters) of the shank with dubbing and bars, five to seven bars total, make a turn forward with the dubbing loop on the shank and let the hackle pliers hang.

Restart the thread on the shank. Bind the end of the dubbing loop and the yarn, and then trim off the ends of loop, yarn, and thread.

10. Consider this when you set out to make the abdomen of your next Brick Back Caddis: You can add the dubbing to the thread heavily, for a thick dubbing loop, or more lightly, for a thinner loop. The less dubbing you spin onto the thread, the longer the loop must be. There's no correct thickness for the loop, so experiment to find what you like. On the left is an abdomen made with a thick dubbing loop, on the right an abdomen from a thinner loop—note that the brown bars up the back are *thicker* on the abdomen built with the *thinner* loop.

11. Find a hackle that, according to your hackle gauge, suits a hook about three sizes larger than yours (example: a size-2 hackle for a size-8 hook). Strip the fluffy fibers from the hackle's base. Strip one side of your hackle from the tip down; bind the hackle, projecting off the hook's eye, just ahead of the body, and then trim off the stem.

12. Wind the hackle *back* in two turns (three at most; try just one sometime) and then spiral the thread *forward* over the stem—this makes the hackle really tough. Find the hackle's tip and trim it out. Pinch the hackle fibers down until they sweep back.

13. Bind a set of pre-made barbell eyes just behind the hook's eye (unless you put a bead on the shank, in which case, no eyes).

14. Make some more sparkling rabbit-and-Mylar dubbing, but in dark-brown this time. (Or just use Arizona Flyfishing's Sparkle Nymph Dubbing in "dark brown.") Dub moderately from the hackles to the eyes, and then around the eyes, with dark dubbing. Whip finish the thread (just behind the hook's eye), trim it, and then add head cement to the whip finish. Brick Back Caddis completed.

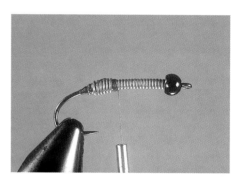

15. Here is how I normally weight a Brick Back Caddis with a metal-bead head. The whole point behind adding the metal bead is to create a fly that sinks fast, so I add even more lead wire than usual. I build the first layer of lead from the bend right up to the bead, cut the ends of the lead, and then push the front of the lead-layer right up into the large end of the hole in the bead. Then I wind on and trim the second short lead layer, start the thread, and bind the lead.

16. I then simply tie and complete the fly as before (minus the plastic eyes, and with the final whip finish at the rear of the bead).

Streamers and Bucktails

Big fly, big fish.

Skip and Shawn Bennett consider bucktail and streamer patterns for Pacific salmon.

Even rich tailwater rivers where tiny flies are common–such as Colorado's South Platte–hold promise for a big Marabou Muddler or Edson Tiger.

THE PEACOCK CHENILLE LEECH

HOOK: Heavy wire, 3X long, sizes 8 and 6.

THREAD: Black 8/0 or 6/0.

BEAD: Gold, 1/8-inch diameter.

TAIL: Black marabou, two strands of peacock-herl-color Krystal Flash or Flashabou along each side.

BODY: Peacock-herl-color plastic chenille.

When trout first stir from winter's drowsiness in early spring—even late winter, in temperate areas—they find little in the lakes to satisfy their complaining stomachs. Chironomids may hatch during the warmest part of the day, but only briefly. There may be scuds and the occasional displaced mayfly or damselfly nymph, but unless they happen upon a prowling dragonfly nymph they'll find nothing so large and satisfying as a leech.

And the leech is always active, always present—trout focus much of their attention on it until the major insect hatches begin.

All this makes the early season an excellent time for a leech-imitating fly, and one you can depend on is Brian Chan's Peacock Chenille Leech. It's a bright fly—brighter than any real leech—but bright flies often work. This one, I've found, can be counted among those bright flies that do work.

Next to the real leech, Brian's modest fly is stunningly beautiful—the leech is a special kind of ugly. This rubbery, tapeworm-like eyesore makes the cliche' "a face only a mother could love" seem wholly inadequate.

1. Slip a metal bead up the hook's shank to its eye. The small end of the bead's hole should meet the eye. Bind two marabou plumes along the shank. The plumes should extend about a full hook's length. Trim off the butts of the marabou.

2. Bind two strands of Krystal Flash or Flashabou along each side of the tail. Trim off the butts of the strands.

3. Bind some plastic chenille along the shank to the bend. Trim off the short, forward end of the chenille.

4. Advance the thread to the rear of the bead. Wind the chenille up the shank in close turns until it is right up against the bead.

5. Bind the end of the chenille behind the bead, and then trim off the end of the chenille. Add a few more tight thread-turns against the rear of the bead. Whip finish and trim the thread, and then add head cement to the whip finish.

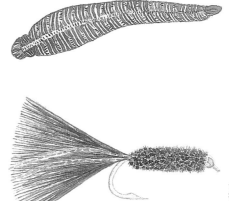

THE HALF AND HALF

HOOK:	Heavy wire, long shank, sizes 4 to 3/0.
THREAD:	Three-ought in a color to blend with the wing's color.
EYES:	Lead barbell eyes (red, usually, with black pupils).
TAIL:	Eight long saddle hackles in two sets with a few strands of Flashabou along the outside of each set. Beneath the saddles, a small bunch of long buck tail.
BODY:	The butts of the buck tail bound up the shank with crisscrossed thread-turns.
WING:	A bunch of long buck tail, usually dark or colored, over light.

As its name suggests, the Half and Half is a blend of about equal parts of two flies: the Clouser Minnow and the Lefty's Deceiver. It's a potent blend. My guide friend Chris Bellows swears by the Half and Half for his ocean salmon fishing out of Neah Bay, Washington. I've used it mainly for largemouth bass, but caught a big cutthroat-rainbow hybrid trout on one up in Canada. Lefty Kreh sent me a letter saying he and Bob Clouser originally developed the Half and Half for big smallmouth bass, but have since found it effective on all sorts of fishes beyond smallmouths. "It is," he says, "a great fly for larger striped bass, excellent on largemouths and a host of other saltwater species." He then adds Northern pike and peacock bass to the list. But once you jiggle-retrieve a Half and Half and watch it shimmy along under water, you won't need testimonials to believe it works.

If you take a reflective look at the Half and Half, and you know the patterns that lent their parts for its creation, you'll see that it was thoughtfully conceived. Probably the most attractive feature of the Clouser Minnow is that it rides with its hook-point up, so that fish are often hooked solidly yet the fly slides freely across rocks, sunken timber and such without snagging (generally). The Half and Half possesses this upturned hook-point. The long tail-wing of the Lefty's Deceiver is likely its best and most distinctive feature—while the forward-mounted feather wing that is standard on streamer flies is notorious for fouling with the hook's bend, the Deceiver's rear-mounted feather tail seldom does. The Half and Half possesses the Deceiver's feather wing-tail.

Top to bottom: Clouser Minnow, Lefty's Deceiver, Half and Half.

The Half and Half is a fly for about any fish looking to eat a smaller fish. Depending on the colors you put in it, it can suggest a number of small fishes and the young of larger fishes. If you make it in some garish, unnatural hue—Chris's favorite is chartreuse—it can imitate nothing yet still catch fish...under the right conditions. I've mostly tied it in fish colors myself—combinations of silver, brown, olive, black, and white. However, in his letter Lefty almost mirrors Chris's preferences: "Two colors have performed best for us on just about every species we have fished...either yellow or white saddle hackles and a chartreuse Clouser upper wing."

I, like most experienced fly tiers, have developed a unique style of tying flies. It's about nuances, mainly. So despite all Lefty's help, it's likely that I tie the Half and Half differently on at least some minor points than he and Bob tie it. That's okay—there is room for personal style in the tying of almost any fly pattern. A fact I find comforting.

RETRIEVES

For largemouth bass, I just toss the Half and Half out near cover, let it sink a little on the weight of its heavy barbell eyes, then twitch and strip it back. It's really just the standard sort of erratic swimming action most fly fishers give any streamer or bucktail fly. Lefty, who has fished the Half and Half for far more species than I have, uses a broad range of retrieves for his fly. He says, "The fly can be retrieved fast or slow," and gives examples: "in shallow water for large and smallmouth bass...the fly is teased slowly along the bottom. For big Northern pike...I like to drop the fly in front of them and retrieve the fly in quick jerks." There's obviously plenty of range here—experiment, until you find what works for the time, place, and species.

LINES

The choice of a fly line really boils down to how deep the fly must go, how quickly it is retrieved (a full-floating line stripped rapidly will draw even the heaviest streamer to the surface), and how heavy its barbell eyes are. In water just a few feet deep, a Half and Half with sufficient weight can stay down on a twitch-and-pause retrieve with a full-floating line. But if the fish are twenty feet down and the fly must race along, a full-sinking, fast-sinking line or dense shooting head is required. So many fishes take the Half and Half under so many conditions that specific recommendations on lines aren't of much value. Just remember that you're trying to keep the fly where the fish want it, keep it moving as the fish prefer, and then choosing a good line will be easy enough.

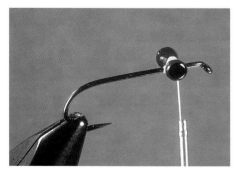

1. Start the thread just behind the hook's eye. Bind some lead or lead-substitute barbell eyes crossways atop the hook's shank—use lot of tight thread-turns to really lock the eyes in place. The eyes should be bound at least 1/8-inch back from the hook's eye.

2. Wind the thread tightly back to the hook's bend. Cup together two sets of long saddle hackles, four in each set. Trim off the hackles' butts, and then bind the hackles all securely atop the bend (or you can bind one bunch on each side, if you find that easier). Bind them by at least 1/8-inch or so of their butts. (The hackles should be long indeed—those on Lefty's sample fly are nearly three times as long as the hook.)

3. Cut a modestly thick but long bunch of buck tail from the hide, hold it by its tips and comb out the short fibers, but do not even the hair's tips in a hair stacker. Spiral the thread up to the rear of the barbell eyes. Bind the butts of the hair there. Spiral the thread down the hair and shank to the hook's bend. Add a few tight thread-turns at the bend. The hair should lie atop the hackles and reach about two thirds down the hackle tail. Trim the butts of the hair closely.

4. About 1/8-inch ahead of the bend, double a few long strands of Flashabou over the thread on one side of the shank. Hold the strands back along the outside of the hackles, and then spiral the thread back to the bend. Add another group of strands along the other side of the shank in the same manner.

5. Spiral the thread back up the shank and buck tail to the barbell eyes. (If you make the spirals even, and match their width to that of the first spirals going *down* the shank, you'll get a neat thread pattern over the body.)

Advance the thread to the front of the eyes. Invert the hook, so that it is now bend-up. Bind a bunch of long light-colored buck tail (not evened in a hair stacker) atop the shank in front of the barbell eyes. (Since the hook is inverted, what is normally considered the underside is now the "top.") The tips of this hair-bunch should reach about two thirds down the hackles.

6. Bind a second bunch of long buck tail (unstacked) over the first; this bunch is usually darker than the first. This top bunch of hair should match the length of the previous bunch. Trim the butts of all the wing hair to a taper, and then bind the butts completely to create a tapered thread head. Whip finish the thread, trim it. Remove the fly from your vise, hold it vertically so that its Flashabou strands hang straight down, and then trim the strands slightly uneven just past the tips of the hackles. Add head cement to the thread head.

STREAMERS AND BUCKTAILS FOR SPRING STREAMS

Carol Ann Morris

With few insects hatching and the rest hiding from the cold, heavy runoff of springtime streams, it is a good bet that the hungry trout in those streams will go for something as big and meaty as a small fish, which the fly fisher can imitate with a streamer or bucktail fly. It is a good bet, to be sure, but I can't quite be sure about much concerning the whole streamer-bucktail thing myself—this is one of those situations in which I know the flies well, but the fishing of them in only a spotty, incomplete way.

Not that I haven't fished bucktails and streamers—I've fished them frequently over the past few decades for smallmouth bass, pan fish, sea-run cutthroat trout, Pacific salmon, largemouth bass, striped bass, and others. And I've fished such flies for resident trout in streams too, just not often enough to really see the patterns.

So I'll turn to others for information on the fishing, and handle the tying in my own way.

In his *New Streamside Guide*, Art Flick voices the standard perspective on streamer and bucktail fishing in speaking of his Black-Nose Dace bucktail: "About the only time I fish it is early in the spring, and on days later in the season when I can do nothing with dry flies." He describes the black-nose dace as the fish that he's found in trout's stomachs more than "all of the other species of minnows combined" in his eastern streams. "Early in the spring" *is* the standard time for bucktails and streamers in trout streams, and after that, like Flick, most anglers only go to baitfish-imitating flies when their favorite methods fail.

But perhaps that's wrong. Perhaps these flies are a sound choice throughout the season. And Flick himself suggests in the *Guide* that he could profit by spending more time fishing "other types of lures," though he goes on to say that something about the dry fly had gotten into his blood. Joe Brooks devotes several pages of his book *Trout Fishing* to streamer fishing in autumn trout streams—Brooks apparently lacked Flick's intrusion of the blood or was strong enough to resist it. In any case, Brooks clearly felt that spring wasn't the only good time for baitfish-imitations and trout.

Yet streamers and bucktails and spring do seem an especially sound match. In spring, trout often move to the edges of a stream to avoid the powerful currents of snow melt and rain—currents which are both tiring and, with all they might dislodge and toss about, even dangerous. The edges are where the tiny fishes

live—if they lived out with full-grown trout there would, of course, *be* no tiny fishes. So this high-water of springtime puts the trout in close proximity to the tiny fishes that streamers and bucktails mimic. And those swift shifting currents may also sweep the tiny fishes out deeper than they'd like. Deeper than they may survive, if the trout are alert. Good conditions for Flick's bucktail fly.

But Art Flick's Black-Nose Dace is only one among thousands—if not tens of thousands—of fish-imitating trout flies. In this article, however, we'll limit the subject to just a few standards with impeccable records, such as the Black-Nose Dace. And the Muddler Minnow.

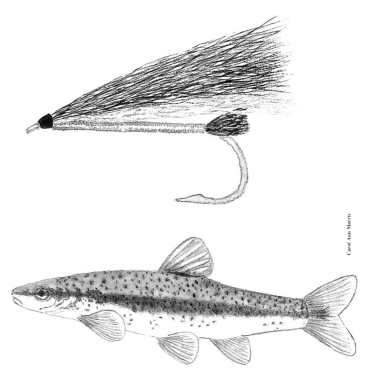

Carol Ann Morris

For several decades, despite the coming and going of many baitfish-imitations, the Muddler Minnow has remained a popular western streamer. Jack Dennis, in his *Western Trout Fly Tying Manual*, says that on big hooks the Muddler imitates a sculpin— a broad-mouthed, dull-colored little bottom-loving fish with a great, flat head—and that in his opinion, the Muddler is "the greatest fly ever tied." Such high praise stems, in part, from how an unweighted Muddler can be fished as a dry fly to loosely imitate all sorts of large floating insects. But the Muddler as sculpin seems to be Jack's favorite use for his favorite fly, since he goes on to describe several ways of fishing it as such.

Generally, fish-imitating flies are classed as "streamers," with wings of long, pliant feathers called hackles, or "bucktails" which have wings of hair, usually, as the name suggests, hair from the tail of a buck deer. The Muddler is an anomaly among streamers and bucktails because it has a wing of both hair *and* feathers, and because of its great hair head—but it's one devil of a popular anomaly.

Dave Whitlock's Whitlock Sculpin is a rather precise imitation of a sculpin, a sort of updated Muddler Minnow.

The Edson Tigers, both light and dark, are true bucktail flies with wings of hair from the tail of a buck. The Tigers are also the only true "attractor" flies here, flies that imitate nothing in particular. Oh sure, trout must sometimes see them darting like fish and take them on the assumption that fish is just what they are. But you needn't look long at either Tiger to start wondering what fish those could possibly be. That's common enough with attractor flies—a rough resemblance to some of the living things on which fish feed, but with no specific model.

If some particular small fish is common to your trout streams—the black-nose dace, the sculpin, the fry of trout...—it makes perfect sense to prefer specific imitations of it. But don't discount the attractor bucktails and streamers—for reasons unknown to man, they are sometimes more effective than imitative flies.

And it's not hard to imagine how attracted a trout would be to a meaty little fish...or an imitation of one.

MUDDLER MINNOW   *Don Gapen*
WEIGHT: Lead wire wound up the shank (optional).
HOOK: Heavy wire, long shank, size 12 to 2.
THREAD: White or gray 8/0, 6/0, or 3/0. (I switch to size-A rod thread for the head.)
TAIL: A single section of mottled-brown turkey primary.
BODY: Flat gold tinsel. (Or braided tinsel, one layer only.)
WING: Brown calf tail inside wings of mottled-brown turkey primary. (Three of my pattern books each give different hairs for the wing—the calf as here, gray squirrel tail, and black and white bear. All work just fine, of course.)
HEAD and COLLAR: Natural-gray deer hair.

BLACK-NOSE DACE   *Art Flick*
HOOK: Heavy wire, 3X or 4X long, sizes 10 to 4.
THREAD: Black 8/0, 6/0, or 3/0.
TAIL: Red yarn.
BODY: Flat silver tinsel.
WING: Brown over dyed-black over white buck tail. (Flick used natural black bear and white polar bear hairs originally, but those are hard to come by now, as perhaps they should be—but he did use buck tail for the brown.)

WHITLOCK SCULPIN   *Dave Whitlock*
HOOK: Heavy wire, 3X or 4X long, sizes 8 to 5/0.
THREAD: Ivory 3/0. (I prefer size-A for the hair head.)
WEIGHT: Lead wire in wrappings under the body.
RIB: Medium-thick gold wire. (I prefer fine copper wire.)
BODY: Pale-yellow or cream dubbing.
BACK and TAIL: Six to eight cree Chinese cock neck hackles, bound with the rib in Matuka-style. (I substituted barred ginger hackles in the fly shown in the photos.)
PECTORAL FINS: Two barred breast feathers from a hen mallard, hen pheasant, or prairie chicken.
GILLS: Red dubbing over the thread-turns securing the pectoral fins.
HEAD and COLLAR: White or cream deer hair below, golden brown topped with black above.

EDSON TIGER, DARK
William R. Edson

HOOK: Heavy wire, 3X or 4X long, sizes 10 to 4.
THREAD: Black 8/0, 6/0, or 3/0.
TAG: Flat gold tinsel.
TAIL: Yellow hackle fibers.
BODY: Medium-diameter yellow chenille.
THROAT: Yellow hackle fibers.
WING: Natural-brown buck tail dyed yellow, a yellowish brown overall.
CHEEKS: Two jungle cock eyes, one on each side. Cheeks are optional on the Edsons and most other streamers and bucktails.

EDSON TIGER, LIGHT
William R. Edson

HOOK: Heavy wire, 3X or 4X long, sizes 10 to 4.
THREAD: Black 8/0, 6/0, or 3/0.
TAG: Flat gold tinsel.
TAIL: Barred wood-duck flank fibers.
BODY: Peacock herl.
WING: Two red hackle-tips or a bunch of red hackle-fibers over dyed-yellow buck tail (natural white buck tail dyed yellow, a true yellow).
CHEEKS: Two jungle cock eyes, one on each side. Optional.

TYING THE BLACK-NOSE DACE

1. Here is how to tie the Black-Nose Dace. Start the thread well up the hook's shank, and then bind some wool yarn from there to the hook's bend. Spiral the thread up the shank. Trim off the front end of the yarn.

2. Trim the end of the yarn tail, short. Bind some flat tinsel along the shank to the bend. Spiral the thread up to hang just behind the hook's eye. Wind the tinsel in close turns up the shank. Bind and then trim the tinsel just back from the eye.

3. Cut, comb, and stack a small bunch of natural-white buck-tail hair. Bind the hair firmly atop the hook just behind the eye.

TYING THE MUDDLER MINNOW

4. Cut, comb, and stack a small bunch of black buck tail; then bind it atop the white. The tips of all the hair should be even. Cut, comb, and stack a small bunch of brown buck tail and bind it atop the black. The resulting hair wing should be about 1 1/2 to 2 times the length of the shank

5. Trim the butts of the hair closely, bind them, and build and complete a thread head.

1. Start the thread about three quarters up the shank. Bind a section from a mottled turkey primary, about half as wide as the hook's gape, along the shank to the bend. The section's long edge should be down and that edge should project from the bend a distance equal to the width of the gape.

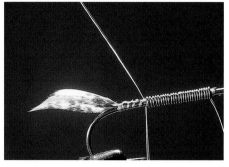

2. Wind a layer of lead wire from a little ahead of the bend to about two thirds of the way up the shank. Cut the ends of the wire closely, press them down flush with the rest of the lead, and then bind the turns of wire with tight turns of thread. Build a little dubbing (any dubbing, really) at the rear end of the lead as a transition from lead to shank.

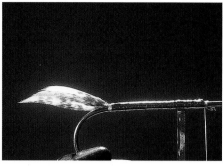

3. Bind some flat gold tinsel two thirds up the shank. Wind the tinsel in close turns back to the tail. Continue winding the tinsel but *forward* now. Bind the tinsel with a few tight thread-turns at the very front of the lead. Trim the end of the tinsel.

4. A few hints for step 3. If you are using Mylar tinsel, it can help to pull the tinsel tight, so that it molds around the irregularities of the foundation—this locks the tinsel in place. And adding a thin layer of head cement or other glue over the foundation before wrapping the first layer of tinsel will *really* lock the tinsel down.

5. Cut, comb, and stack a small bunch of calf tail. Bind the calf atop the front of the tinsel body with tight turns of thread. The tips of the calf should reach back to the bend but no farther than the tip of the tail.

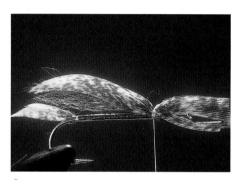

6. Cut sections from a matched pair (left and right) of mottled-brown turkey primaries. The sections should be as wide as the tail or slightly wider. Cup the sections around the hair bunch. Bind the sections securely with tight thread-turns and then trim the butts closely. The sections should be long-edge down, and should reach to the bend but no farther than the tip of the tail.

7. Wind the thread out ahead of the front of the body a few turns, and then whip finish it there. Trim the thread. Start some size-A rod-winding thread over the whip finish. Cut, comb, and stack a modest bunch of deer hair. Push the hair down around the shank just in front of the body. The evened tips of the hair should project rearward about halfway down the body (or slightly farther).

8. Take two light-tension turns of thread around the hair and then, holding the hair firmly in place, pull the thread tight. Still holding the thread tight, draw back the hair butts, pull the thread sharply forward, and add several tight turns of thread on the bare shank right in front of the hair.

9. Compress the hair back with a hair-packing tool or your thumb and finger. Flare another bunch of hair as before, in front of the first bunch. The tips of this second bunch needn't be stacked. Compress this second bunch back into the first. Add another bunch, if necessary. On most hooks, two bunches of compressed hair should cover the front third of the shank for the hair head, but add a third bunch if needed.

10. Whip finish the thread at the eye and trim it closely. Add head cement to the whip finish now or after the head is trimmed. With scissors or a razor blade (handle a razor blade carefully!), trim the head to a tapered and flattened shape. Leave most or all of the hair-tip collar intact.

The logical shape for a Muddler head is flattened, and rounded across the top, though you'll see lots of variations.

THE LEFTY'S DECEIVER

HOOK:	Heavy wire, short shank to standard length (rust- and corrosion-resistant for saltwater); Lefty gauges hook-size by fly-length, and fly-length runs from 2 1/2 inches to over a foot.
THREAD:	Three-ought, usually dark.
TAIL (wing):	Two sets of saddle hackles.
CHEEKS:	Buck tail.
TOPPING:	Buck tail, sometimes peacock herl or synthetic strands, or any combination of these.
THROAT:	Flashabou or Krystal Flash (sometimes rabbit fur).
EYES:	Any paint that won't react with epoxy glue.

Just another streamer fly, you'd assume, same old materials, same old form. But you'd be wrong—the Lefty's Deceiver has a few unusual twists in its design, one in particular hidden at its very core. Here are a few of those twists:

First, the wing is actually the tail.

Second, the bright strands terminating at various points along its sides are uncommon on streamers (or at least they were uncommon until the Deceiver hit its stride).

Third, thick tufts of hair form elongated cheeks at the sides.

Fourth (and to me, most interesting of all), the fly is built in two well-spaced sections that blend to the unified look, as they should, of a small fish.

There is sound logic behind all these unconventional features. The wing as tail is a practical way to create a wing unlikely to foul in the bend of the hook. The bright trailing strands make sense in a fly intended to match bright-scaled fishes, and their varied lengths probably smooth out the effect. The hair-tuft cheeks add thickness that most streamers lack, so that when fish view a Deceiver from above or below, as they sometimes must, it looks properly properly filled out. And the final anomaly—the two-section design—was probably just the result of working out some of the aforementioned features.

Lefty Kreh, an author of fly-fishing books, whose Southern charm and sly wit have raised him to the top of the speaking circuit, originally developed his Deceiver for the striped bass of Chesapeake Bay. That was in the early 1960s. Encouraged by its success there, he began trying it on all sorts of saltwater fishes. It seemed to appeal to them all. Today the Lefty's Deceiver is tied and fished, in Lefty's words, "in lengths from 2 1/2 inches to more than a foot" long. It has become a standard for nearly all saltwater fishes, and Eric Leiser, in *The Book of Fly Patterns*, includes "some of our larger freshwater species" as additional targets. Lefty once told me that an all-black version of his Deceiver had caught on as a fly for largemouth bass, especially in colored water. So I tied up a few and tried them in my darker local bass lakes.

The bass relished them, of course.

A few points on tying the Deceiver. First, Lefty advises that the tail-wing should be of saddle, *not* neck *hackles. Second, he recommends at least three* pairs *of hackles for that wing, more than three on for the largest hooks. And third, make sure those hackle pairs curve in together (like the hackles on the yellow-and-green Deceiver at the top of the photo), are "cupped", to produce the impression of a fish when viewed from top or bottom.*

There are many variations of this versatile fly that Lefty describes as, rather than a concrete pattern, "a style or type of fly." In his book Salt Water Fly Patterns, *Lefty lists some alternative materials: marabou or fisHair for the tail-wing, various feathers for cheeks, peacock herl as a topping... In the book he lists 18 specific Deceiver patterns but makes it clear that they are "only some of the basic combinations." As I said, versatile fly.*

1. Start the thread at the hook's bend. Set three to five slender saddle hackles together, curves matching, tips evened. Build another hackle-set, same number of hackles. Place one hackle-set up against the other, cupped together, tips evened. Trim the butts of the hackles and then bind them all, by their stems, atop the bend. The hackles should project from the bend about two full hook-lengths.

2. Bind about ten strands of Flashabou or Krystal Flash at the bend, along one side of the hackles. Bind another ten strands along the other side. Trim the butts of the strands and then bind them thoroughly.

3. Trim the strands to varied lengths—some fully as long as the hackles, others only half as long, the rest in between.

4. Advance the thread in close turns to just back from the hook's eye, perhaps 1/8-inch. Snip a bunch of buck tail from the hide, and then bind it along one side of the hook, near the eye. (Do not even the buck tail in a hair stacker.) The longest hairs should extend about halfway down the hackles. Bind a second bunch along the other side.

5. Trim and bind the butts of the buck tail. Bind some longer buck tail (again, no stacking) atop the hook behind the eye, over the hackles. This bunch should extend about three quarters down the fly. As shown here, a second bunch of fibers (Krystal Flash, in this case) is sometimes bound atop the buck tail. Trim the butts of all this topping, and then trim (if necessary) the synthetic fibers about three-quarters down the fly.

6. Invert the hook (by removing it and then mounting it again upside down in the jaws, or, with a rotary vise, by simply rotating the jaws). Bind 10 to 15 strands of Flashabou or Krystal Flash atop the hook's shank just behind the eye as a throat. Trim and bind the butts of the strands; then trim the strands to length—just short of the hook's point.

7. Build and whip finish a thread head; then trim the thread. Paint eyes on the sides of the head. When the paint is dry, coat the head and eyes with epoxy glue (*glue*, not epoxy *finish* as used in rod-making).

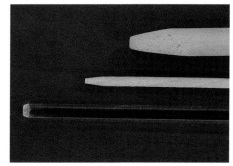

8. Many use round, blunt dowels—wood, plastic, whatever—for making the eyes. (I use standard water-base poster paints.) Just push the paint-coated point of the dowel straight into the head; then back the dowel off, leaving a spot of paint. Use a slimmer dowel for the pupils.

THE ZONKER IN GENERAL,
AND A VARIATION IN PARTICULAR

BABY BASS ZONKER

HOOK: Heavy wire, 3X to 6X long, sizes 10 to 2.
THREAD: Brown or dark-olive 3/0 for both ends.
WEIGHT: Lead wire (optional).
BODY: Gold Mylar piping. (The original Zonker has a piece of adhesive metal tape folded over the hook's shank and trimmed to a rounded shape; the Mylar piping goes over that. I like the Zonker better without the metal tape.)
TAIL: The end of the body Mylar.
COLLAR: Grizzly hackle dyed olive (a hen neck; soft rooster saddle; or big, soft dry-fly neck hackle).
BACK and TOP of TAIL: A strip of dark-olive rabbit hide with fur.

You could say that I didn't take well to production fly tying. After a few hours of it my sense of reality would weaken, and I'd drift into a surreal place where patches of long saddle hackle became tentacled creatures and my tying vise an obstinate robot refusing to firmly hold a hook, then wrestling me for possession of it. A mechanical arm held an illuminated cone that shone down onto the robot-vise. The arm would lower the cone, just slightly (it was an old lamp, and the joint was always slipping)—I knew then that it was posturing for a strike, that the cone would snap to my heart and suck life's essence from my trembling body as a spider sucks life from a terrified fly.

Then the cat would jump into my lap and I would, of course, let go a howl.

During my stint as a production tier I experienced many of these bizarre episodes, and tied a whole lot of a fly called a Zonker. By the time I gave up production tying (for the sake of my mental health), I had worked out a good many details about the tying of this unusual fly.

I first heard the word "Zonker" uttered in a fly shop in the early 1980s, and I've been tying Zonkers and fishing them ever since. They've taken all sorts of fish for me—pan fish of several species, smallmouth bass, three or four of the trouts and chars, and probably a couple of fishes I can't now recall. But mostly I've fished them for largemouth bass. Tied with a gold body and a dark-olive or dark-brown back, the Zonker becomes a fine imitation of a standard prey of an adult bass: a baby bass. And I've seen largemouths feeding on their babies often enough to know that those babies are worth imitating.

So I make it move like a baby bass—make it glide and dart and jiggle. And I usually fish it in the shallows, where a baby bass eludes its carnivorous parents.

Sometimes I fish a Zonker with a white back. It appears, just a foot or so down, as a pale smear, stretching to swim and spreading on a pause. When the white *dis*appears, I strike.

My Baby Bass version of the Zonker varies from the original only in color, and is therefore not really my own pattern. Tying style is another matter—and that which follows is all mine, though it's only fair to add that bits of it were collected from others. Please give my style consideration; I paid a dear price for it—a decade of experimentation at the vise and on the water and many visits to a surreal and unsettling place.

The Zonker was created by extrovert Dan Byford, who makes his living in ways unusual even in the world of fly tying. To know Dan is to know that he, of all fly tiers, would be the likeliest to name a fly *Zonker*.

The author with a Zonker-caught bass (which was released immediately after shutter went off).

Carol Ann Morris

A white-back Zonker.

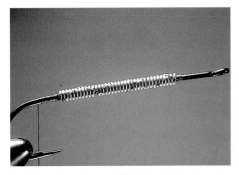

1. Start the thread tightly at the hook's bend. Wrap a layer of lead wire up the hook's shank from 1/4 inch ahead of the bend to at least 1/8 inch back from the hook's eye. Trim the ends of the wire, and then bind it with tight thread-turns. (Adding lead at all, by the way, is optional.) End with the thread hanging at the bend.

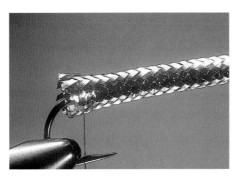

2. Cut a length of Mylar tubing slightly longer than the hook. Pull the core out of the tubing. Slide the tubing over the eye and down the shank. The very end of the tubing usually unravels from cutting and handling, but if it didn't, unravel it. Slip that unraveled end slightly past the hanging thread.

3. Take a couple of loose thread-turns around the Mylar; then hold the Mylar firmly in place and pull the thread tight. The Mylar should now be locked in place. Add a few tight thread-turns to really secure everything.

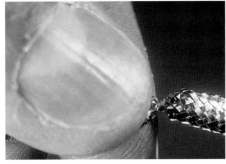

4. Take up another bobbin loaded with the same thread. With your right hand (right-hander's instructions), grasp the Mylar at the eye and push it back lightly. This fills out the body. Grasp the Mylar with your left hand, just back from the eye. Take up that second bobbin in your right hand, and then start the thread over the Mylar, just back from eye. This is a bit tricky—you'll have to hold both the Mylar and the free end of the thread in your left hand—but it gets easy with practice.

5. Add several tight thread-turns over the end of the Mylar. Trim the free end of the thread you just started, and then trim the Mylar back from the eye. Push the trimmed, secured end of the Mylar back, so that it slides down the shank a little, to make room for the hackle and head.

6. Select a hackle. The best way I know to do this is to stroke a few fibers perpendicular to a hackle's stem, then measure the fibers against the hook. I prefer that the fibers are about half the total length of the hook.

7. Advance the thread to just back from the eye. Strip the fluffy fibers from the base of the hackle. Bind on the hackle projecting forward, over the eye. End with the thread back against the front of the body. Trim the hackle's stem closely.

8. Wind the hackle *back* in close turns to the front of the body. At least four turns, and as many as eight—a matter of personal preference.

9. Secure the tip of the hackle with a turn or two of thread; then spiral the thread *forward* through the hackle to the eye.

10. Find and snip out the hackle's tip. Stroke the fibers back and squeeze them down flat against the body. Hold the fibers back as you wind tight thread-turns back over them—but only wrap back a little, a distance about equal to the width of the eye.

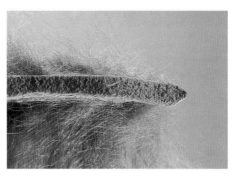

11. Trim the end of a 1/8-inch-wide "Zonker" strip, a strip of rabbit hide with fur, to a short point. (The fur should cant *down* the strip, not across it as on a "cross-cut rabbit" strip.) The fur should cant away from the point you just cut.

12. Bind on the strip by its point just behind the hook's eye. Use plenty of tight thread-turns creating, finally, a tapered thread-head. Wet the fur for control, if needed. Whip finish and trim the thread.

13. Stretch the strip *lightly* back over the body. With a bodkin or the tips of your scissors, part the hair directly over the thread-turns at the bend. Dampen the hair to keep it parted. Add lots of tight thread-turns over the hide strip. Take several turns over a loop of fine monofilament (tippet). Cut the thread long; then slip its cut end through the loop. Hold the end of the thread as you pull the loop back out through the thread-turns, pulling the free end of the thread through with it. Trim the thread closely.

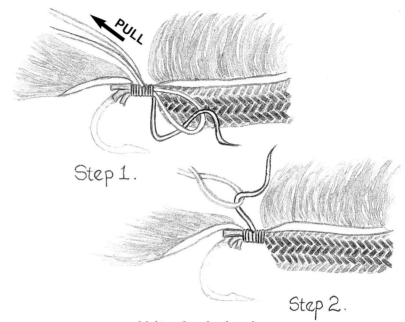

Making fast the thread-turns.

Carol Ann Morris

14. Trim the strip's hide at the bend—directly over the far edge of the bend is good. (Trim it to a point if you like.) Add head cement to both the thread head and the band of thread at the bend.

15. I often find that my rabbit fur is too long for smaller hooks. My remedy: trim the hair along the back.

Note that this Zonker also has a snag guard, which at times is a blessing.

16. Here's the original Zonker pattern:

HOOK: Heavy wire, long shank, sizes 8 to 2.
THREAD: Black 3/0 for both ends.
BODY: Silver Mylar piping.
COLLAR: One grizzly hackle.
TAIL: The ends of the body-Mylar.
WING and TOP of TAIL: A natural-gray Zonker strip.

Bass and Pan-Fish Flies

A largemouth bass.

A big bluegill.

*Hunting smallmouth bass on the
Susquehanna River in Pennsylvania.*

Skip casts a hair bug to shallow largemouth bass.

TAP'S BUG

HOOK:	Heavy wire, wide gape (standard bass-fly hook), in the standard size-range.
THREAD:	Heavy hair-flaring thread—size-A rod-winding, flat waxed nylon, Kevlar—whatever kind you prefer. (I like size-D rod-thread myself.)
TAIL (and the rear of the body):	Deer hair.
BODY:	Deer hair.

In the April/May 1998 issue of *Warmwater Fly Fishing* magazine, William Tapply chronicles the development of and theories behind the Tap's Bug. He should know—his father, H.G. "Tap" Tapply, who wrote the column "Tap's Tips" in *Field and Stream* for 35 years, created the fly. His father Tap, he says, was and is a "compulsive tinkerer." Tapply, the younger, then describes how Tapply, the elder, refined his fly through a long process of experimentation and testing (and, I assume, "tinkering").

All this fooling around to smooth out the details of so simple a fly as the Tap's Bug may seem silly to some. But not to me. I've designed a few fly patterns, and each took at least a year to develop, probably three years on average. And one of my big gripes is the fly pattern that's conceived in one impulsive swipe at the tying vise, "tested" by just one showing to the fish, and then heralded as the new miracle fly in a magazine article. So I say hats off to Tap for taking the time and investing the effort to get his fly right.

In *Bassin' with a Fly Rod*, author Jack Ellis describes the Tap's Bug as "an incredibly basic, and quite effective, version of the hair bug." Dick Stewart and Farrow Allen, in *Flies for Bass & Panfish*, call it "a reliable standard." Apparently, Tap did get his bug right.

Here are a few of Skip's tips for tying the Tap's Bug (most of which are tips from William Tapply's article that are actually tips from his father, Tap, who wrote "Tap's Tips"). Tip #1: find the right deer hair for the tail. You need long hair, fine throughout most of its length yet thick and spongy at the butt. The tips make the tail, the butts flare as part of the body. (I have tied this fly with buck tail for the tail and deer hair flared for the body, and the bass overlooked my faux pas; still, if you want the fly tied as its creator intended...) Tip #2: form a flat face on the fly. Tap says that "a flat-faced deer-hair bug plows through the water and burbles...and it seems to drive bass nuts." "Burbling," he feels, is subtle, and more effective than the violent crack typical of a cork popper, which he says "is just as likely to spook a bass as attract him." The Tap's Bug is otherwise such a simple fly that these two tips should suffice.

Tap ties his fly on size 2/0 hooks for largemouth bass and size-1 hooks for smallmouth. I, myself, often tie it on smaller hooks for both species—the largemouths of my local lakes run small, as do the smallmouths where I fish for them most often.

Regarding color, Tap seems open to just about any combination, but does prefer a face of white or yellow to make the fly stand out on the water. I have seen the orange-black-yellow combination often enough that I suspect it's become the standard. Still, at times a somber or dark bug is just what bass prefer, and since Tap seems flexible about colors...

The Tap's Bug is utter simplicity, and its uncluttered form makes it easier to cast than bass bugs with widely spread legs and waving rubber arms. And bass like it. That's good enough for me.

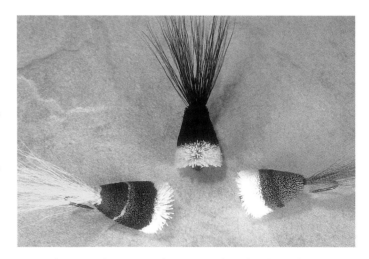

Tap's Bugs of various colors. Some have buck tail for tails, others have long, fine deer-hair tails whose butts were flared to become part of the body, in Tap's tying style.

1. Start the heavy thread near the hook's bend. Cut a bunch of long, fine-tipped, thick-butted deer hair from right next to the hide. Comb out the butts of the deer and then even the tips in a hair stacker. Work the butts of the hair down around the hook's shank a little, take two turns of thread around the hair, and pull the thread tight. The tips of the hair should project about a full hook's length beyond the bend.

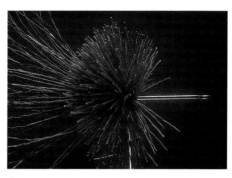

2. Draw back the butts of the hair, pull the thread firmly forward through the hair, and then add a few tight thread-turns or a half hitch to lock the thread in place. I then like to add a second bunch of hair in the same color as the first.

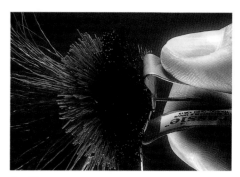

3. Flare a hair-bunch or two of another color ahead of the first bunches. Always compress each new bunch back into the previous bunches. You can accomplish this with your thumb and forefinger or a hair-packing tool.

4. There are no rules as to how many colors you can use in a Tap's Bug: three seems most common, but one, two, four, more—almost anything goes. However, if the last bunch or two is white or yellow, the bug will be easy to see on water. When all the hair is flared and compressed along the shank, whip finish the thread (or add several half hitches) and trim it.

5. As with nearly all flared-hair flies, cut first along the underside until you can see the hook's bend. Then, using the bend as a guide, complete a flat underside that is fairly close to the shank.

6. With scissors or a razor blade, shape the sides and top of the bug; then round the top half while leaving the underside flat—the result is more or less a half-circle in cross section.

7. Tap prefers that the bug's face be flat. This may result from simply leaving the face uncut. But if you packed the hair really tightly, it may project forward and require trimming.

Complete the Tap's bug by coating the whip finish (or half hitches) with head cement.

THE SILVER OUTCAST

HOOK: Heavy wire, short to regular shank, standard bass-streamer sizes.

THREAD: Black 8/0, 6/0/, or 3/0.

BODY: Flat silver tinsel.

WING: White buck tail under blue buck tail under yellow buck tail. A few strands of peacock herl atop all the buck tail.

Though I probably know all I need to about Charles Waterman's Silver Outcast, a streamer fly for bass, I'd like to know more. I'd like to know, for example, on what style of hook this fly should be tied. I'd like to know how small to how large that hook should run. And should the Outcast have jungle-cock eyes (my assortment of fly-pattern books show it both with and without)? And where in blazes is that pestiferous bunch of blue buck tail supposed to be positioned in the wing?

These technical questions really taunt me—I like to have all the details that leave no doubts about how a particular fly pattern is tied. Soon, I'm playing with variations, conducting my little experiments, but I need a solid foundation of concrete facts from which to launch my flights of imagination. So I spent some time with Waterman's book, *Black Bass & the Fly Rod*, and some others and came up with the answers—or, rather, best guesses—that follow: The hook should be of heavy wire and regular length or short shank. Hook-size seems to be a personal matter, though large hooks seem standard. Jungle-cock eyes are optional, but

adding eyes to a streamer always makes sense because such flies normally suggest small fish. And the blue buck tail probably belongs in the middle, between the bunches of white and yellow (even though *Flies for Bass & Panfish*, by Dick Stewart and Farrow Allen, shows a sample Outcast with the blue on top).

That's probably all about right, though a bit speculative. On the other hand, I *do* know a few things about the Silver Outcast for certain. I know that Waterman developed the fly by accident—his rendering of a fly called the Silver Doctor was somehow so far off the mark that when Dan Bailey saw the aberrant version he said, according to Waterman, that it "didn't look like any Silver Doctor he ever produced at his fly shop." I know that it's always been considered primarily a fly for large-mouth and smallmouth bass. And I know that as bass flies go, it's an easy one to tie, and easy to cast.

I also know that it works.

So I suppose that even though I'd like more hard, sure details about the Silver Outcast, I know enough.

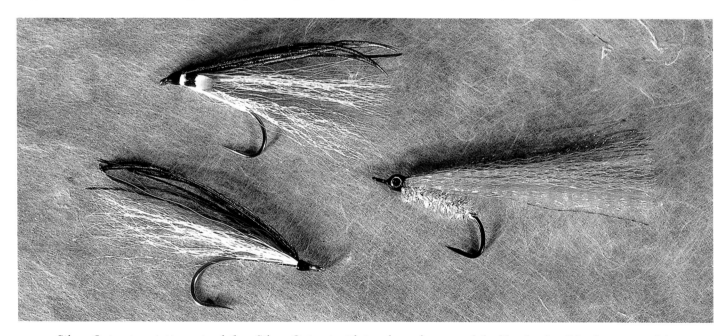

Silver Outcast variations: top left, a Silver Outcast with jungle cock eyes and the blue buck tail in the center of the wing; lower left, another Outcast with no eyes and the blue buck tail over the yellow; on the right, an Outcast of all synthetic materials, an idea Skip got from editor Art Scheck.

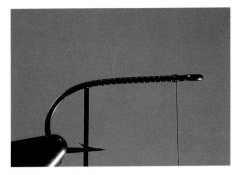

1. Start the thread just back from the hook's eye; trim the end of the thread. Bind on some flat silver tinsel (or two-color Mylar tinsel with the silver side up) just back from the eye. Wind the tinsel in close tight turns to the hook's bend.

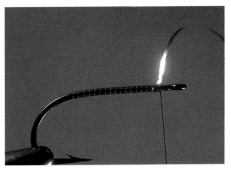

2. Wind the tinsel forward to its starting point, again in tight close turns; secure the tinsel under a few tight thread-turns. Trim both the stub ends of the tinsel.

3. Stack a small bunch of white buck tail, and then bind it just behind the hook's eye. The buck tail should project back, from where it is bound on, about two full hook lengths.

4. Closely trim the butts of the hair and partially bind them. There is more buck tail and a topping of peacock herl remaining to complete this wing, and Waterman says he prefers this wing tied "pretty skimpily," so keep this in mind.

5. Over the white buck tail, bind a small bunch of stacked blue buck tail. The tips of the blue should be even with the tips of the white. Trim the butts of this new bunch and, again, partially bind them.

6. Over the blue buck tail, bind and trim a small bunch of stacked yellow, in the same manner as the previous two bunches.

7. Over the yellow buck tail, bind a small bunch of peacock herl. The tips of the herl should be even; they should also be even with the tips of the buck tail. Trim the butts of the herl closely. Build and complete a thread head to complete the Silver Outcast.

8. Some tiers add cheeks of jungle cock, which suggest eyes. An eyed jungle-cock feather is simply stripped of its fuzzy fibers and bound to one side of the thread head. Then a second jungle-cock feather is bound to the other side before the thread head is completed.

THE McGINTY

HOOK:	Heavy wire, standard length or 1X long, sizes 14 to 10.
THREAD:	Black 8/0 or 6/0.
TAIL:	Barred teal over red hackle fibers.
BODY:	One strand each of black and yellow chenille.
HACKLE:	Brown.
WINGS:	White-tipped mallard secondary quill sections.

There's little doubt as to what inspired the design of the McGinty wet fly—one look will tell you that it came from a bee or wasp or some other portly black-and-yellow-banded buzzer. (There is also a McGinty dry fly, but it's largely gone; when someone says "McGinty" now, he or she is almost certainly referring to the wet-fly version.)

The real doubts about the McGinty concern what, if anything, it imitates. Sure, it looks like a bee (a bee, that is, with white-tipped wings and a long, red-black-white tail in place of a stinger), but I've always read that it's supposed to be fished on a swimming retrieve. So what does *that* imitate? A swimming bee? I think not.

When I discussed this mystery of a fly that mimics appearance but not action with my editor, Art Scheck, he neatly summed the whole thing up. He said: "The McGinty imitates a McGinty."

In other words, it imitates nothing.

But fish like it regardless. Which brings us to the matter of exactly which fishes those would be.

Listed in such trout-fly books as Terry Helleckson's *Popular Fly Patterns* (1976) and Stewart and Allen's *Flies for Trout* (1993), the McGinty would seem to be a trout fly. However, going more on impression and experience than research, I'd say

that while it once was primarily a fly for trout, it now mostly isn't. In the days when practically every fly fisher twitched wet flies in trout streams, the McGinty and a whole lot of other wet flies filled anglers' boxes. Today, only a few old-fashioned wet flies remain popular, and the popularity of one of them, the McGinty, lies almost entirely in the pan-fish realm. Not a new realm at all, however, for the McGinty—in *Lucas on Bass Fishing* published in 1947, Jason Lucas, in his chapter titled "Fly Fishing for Sunfish," says about sunfish flies, "One of my favorites is the McGinty...."

Bluegills—and probably other pan fishes such as green sunfish and pumpkinseeds—do eat bees. I'm not going on impression this time; I'm quoting Jack Ellis, author of *The Sunfishes*. In *Sunfishes* he says: "I see bream (pan fish) taking bees and wasps all the time...." He describes how honey bees and bumble bees gather around the flowering water plants of the South and how in his native East Texas "the shallows are quite literally buzzing with activity from mid-March until the first of May." And: "A size 12 McGinty or my own Bumble McDougal will bring constant rises at this time."

So even though the McGinty is normally twitched just beneath the surface for pan fish, it makes perfect sense to fish it quietly among bluegills and buzzing and floundering bees. Ellis advises us to fish it "without retrieve," to just "jiggle it a little bit." In which case the McGinty actually imitates something. Something, that is, other than a McGinty.

1. Start the thread about three quarters up the hook's shank. Bind a small bunch of hackle fibers atop the shank, where the thread was started. Strip off some barred teal fibers and bind them atop the hackle fibers. Hold all the fibers back and spiral the thread down them and the shank to the hook's bend. The resulting tail should be equal to the full length of the hook.

2. Trim the butts of the tail fibers closely. Bind a length of yellow and a length of black chenille from the bend up three quarters of the shank. The thread should now hang at this three-quarters point. Trim the butts of the chenille. The small-diameter chenille shown above is fine for the range of hook sizes listed in the pattern.

3. Wind the two lengths of chenille forward, side by side, in close turns to the hanging thread. Bind the ends of the chenille and trim them closely.

4. Bind a hen neck hackle by either its tip or stripped butt at the front of the body. Whichever way you bind the hackle, strip the fibers from its butt. The advantage to binding the hackle by its tip is that the fibers will slant neatly back when that hackle is wound. Trim the hackle's tip or stem (whichever is lashed to the hook) closely. The thread should now hang just ahead of the body but just back from the hook's eye.

5. Wind the hackle forward in three to six close turns. Bind the tip or butt of the hackle (whichever is the opposite end from the one you first bound on) and then trim it closely.

6. These are the white-tipped mallard secondary quills from which come the McGinty's wings. A section has been cut from the same part of each matching quill. Do the same with your quills. The quill-section wings should be no wider than the hook's gape; slimmer is fine, too.

7. Bind on the quill-section wings atop the hook at the front of the body. Trim closely the butts of the wings, complete a thread head, trim the thread, and add head cement to the head.

Wing length is somewhat subjective. The wings can be as short as you see them here or as long as on the fly on the previous page. And the long edge of the wings can be down (as here) or up (as on the previous page)—your choice.

Brian Rose

Flies for Atlantic Salmon, Steelhead, Pacific Salmon, and Migratory Trout

Releasing a silver salmon ten miles off the Washington coast.

Oregon's Lower Deschutes River–famous steelhead water.

A sea-run cutthroat trout.

THE BOMBER AND THE GREEN MACHINE

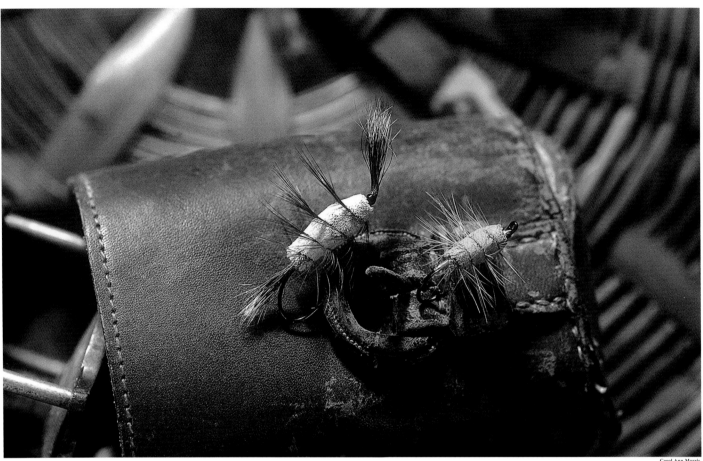

Fly patterns that make a splash usually see their popularity evaporating within a decade, and by the two-decade mark drift only as foggy memories in the backs of most fly fisher's minds. A few, however, endure. The Bomber is among those few.

After thirty to forty years on the scene, this fly still shows up in the catalogs of some big fly-fishing mail-order houses, and those businesses carry only what sells. Clearly the Bomber, after all these years, still sells.

The Bomber first appeared, according to Joseph Bates, Jr. in his book *Atlantic Salmon Flies & Fishing*, "in 1967 for use on New Brunswick's Miramichi River." Though designed for Atlantic salmon, the fly then, says Kent Helvie in his book *Steelhead Fly Tying Guide*, "made its way west and the steelhead fishermen grabbed it up." *The Book of Fly Patterns* by Eric Leiser, published in 1987, describes the Bomber as "one of the most popular salmon dry flies used in Canada."

Bates says that the Bomber is fished "dry, dry and dragging (with a fast skittering motion), or wet with a sinking line." I doubt many Bombers are thrown on sinking lines today, but "dry" and "dry and dragging" are probably as common as ever for Atlantic salmon, and for steelhead.

Then there's the Green Machine, another child of the Miramichi River. Though similar in form to the Bomber—a fat trimmed-hair body with a single hackle spiraled up it—the Green Machine is commonly fished *subsurface*. It is a member of the Wet Bug line of salmon flies and as Dick Talleur explains in his book *The Versatile Fly Tyer*, it appears "at first glance to be a dry fly, and it probably could serve as such, but that's not usually how it's fished." He goes on to say that the Wet Bug series is most effective fished "just beneath the surface or in the film."

Yet even if the Bomber and Green Machine are usually fished differently, they have much in common—both were born on the Miramichi, both were designed for Atlantic salmon, both possess plump bodies of flared-and-shaped deer hair bristling with hackle fibers, and both are tied in about the same manner. And, where one has endured, the other promises equal longevity.

A Bomber dragging across current.

90   MORRIS ON TYING FLIES

TYING TIPS FOR THE BOMBER AND GREEN MACHINE

There are all sorts of approaches for tying these flies, and most of the variations seem to involve the hackle. It's unusual in fly tying to wind a hackle up through a body of flared deer hair—an oddity in a craft in which oddities abound. And the shaping of the body makes getting the hackle mounted and wound even trickier. Talleur binds in the hackle *after* the body if completed; he does so by winding the thread back in wide spirals through the trimmed hair, binding the tip of the hackle down into the hair, winding the thread forward through the hair to the hook's eye, and then winding the hackle as usual. Leiser binds on *two* hackles *before* making the body so that if he accidentally trims off one, another remains for the job. I've used both approaches, and find Talleur's the easier, Leiser's the neater, by just a little. I'll demonstrate with Leiser's method, the one I normally follow.

Regarding how the bodies of the Bomber and Green Machine should be shaped, there seem to be two basic schools: the cigar-shape school, and the weight-forward school. The first advocates the typical cigar's thick center tapering to thinner ends; the second advocates making the thick part the front end of the body. Either shape is good.

BOMBER

HOOK: Slightly heavy to medium wire, up or down eye, 4X long, sizes 8 to 2.

THREAD: Brown or tan 8/0 or 6/0 for the tail, hackle, and wing. Size-A rod-thread for flaring the deer-hair body.

TAIL: Woodchuck guard hair (or substitute calf tail, squirrel tail—any fairly stiff hair).

HACKLE: One, brown (though I like to bind on two, one as a back-up).

WING: The same hair as you used in the tail.

BODY: Natural deer hair. (All sorts of dyed hair colors—sometimes in contrasting bands—are commonly used.)

GREEN MACHINE

HOOK: Slightly heavy to medium wire, sizes 8 to 4.

THREAD: Green 8/0 or 6/0 for the tip, tag, and hackle. Size-A rod-thread for the body.

TIP: Fine silver Mylar tinsel.

TAG: Hot orange or red floss.

HACKLE: One, brown (I bind on two, for insurance).

BODY: Medium-green deer hair.

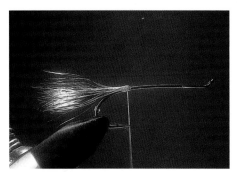

1. Here's how to tie the Bomber. Start the thread at the hook's bend. Cut, comb, and stack a small bunch of woodchuck guard hairs. Trim the butts of the hair straight across. Bind the hair only an eighth-inch or so up from the cut ends of its butts, atop the rear of the hook's shank. The resulting tail should extend a distance between half and two thirds the length of the shank.

2. While holding the tips of two saddle hackles of appropriate size for your hook, stroke some of the fibers back for a little ways up the stems. The point is to get the tips cleared away so that you can bind them over the butt of the tail.

So...bind the tip of the hackles over the butt of the tail.

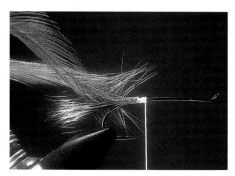

3. Pull the hackles back, whip finish the thread out just ahead of the hair-butts, and then trim the end. Start the size-A thread over the whip finish you just made. The size-A should be directly in front of the tail.

4. Trim a pencil-thick bunch of deer hair from the hide. Hold the hair by the tips as you stroke out the short hairs and fuzz with any sort of comb. Trim the butts again, for a clean edge, and then set the hair down atop the hook's shank. The cut edge of the hair should be at the rear of the thread-windings and the bulk of the hair should project over the eye.

5. While holding the thread securely, take two light-tension turns of thread around the hair; work the hair down around the shank a little; and then pull the thread tight (from one side, then the other, to keep the hair centered). When you're finished, it should look like this.

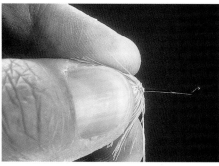

6. Pull the front-hair firmly back, pull the thread firmly forward, and then take four or five tight turns of thread in front of the hair.

7. Continue flaring hair up the shank to just back from the eye. Compress each flared bunch back into the last using thumb and forefinger or a hair-packing tool. Make several tight half hitches in the thread behind the eye; then cut the thread.

8. With razor blade or scissors, trim the body to a not-*too*-thick cigar sort of shape. Watch out for the hackles—trim them off and you have a real problem! (But if you do, the best solution is to bind a hackle in after the body is trimmed using Dick Talleur's method I described previously in this article.)

9. Restart the finer thread at the eye. There, bind another bunch of the same hair you used for the tail. This wing-hair should also be stacked and bound only by a short length of the hair butts, and should be about the same length as the tail.

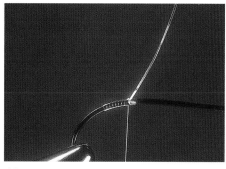

10. Take up a hackle and wind it up the body. Be sure to use enough tension to pull the hackle well down into the hair—but not so much tension that you break the stem. Four to six turns of hackle is the normal range. Bind the hackle's stem at the front of the body with a few thread-turns, whip finish the thread, trim its end, and add head cement to the whip finish to complete the Bomber.

11. Here is how to tie the Green Machine. Start the thread up the shank a bit from the bend (directly over the hook's point is just right on most hooks). Bind on the end of some flat Mylar tinsel with the silver side up. (Such tinsel is usually gold on one side, silver on the other.) Wind the tinsel in close turns to the hook's bend, then back to its starting point. Bind the end of the tinsel there and then trim both its ends.

12. Bind on the end of some floss at the upper end of the tinsel. Wrap the floss back over most of the tinsel. When only two or three turns of tinsel lie exposed, wind the floss forward again to its starting point. Bind the end of the floss, and then trim both its ends.

From here, it's just like tying a Bomber without a wing (or tail)—bind on the hackles, flare and shape the body, spiral a hackle forward, build and complete a tapered thread head.

The Miramichi River.

THREE NEW FLIES FOR SEA-RUNS

Upon hearing the words "salt water," most fly fishers melt into a dreamy look, their minds lost in reveries of tropical breezes across bonefish flats, enormous tarpon twisting up in midair leaps, postcard stuff. That's *most* fly fishers, but not necessarily those here in the Pacific Northwest. Sure, a good many of us in Western Washington and Western Oregon fish tropical waters, but having a vast coastline at our doorstep that is haunted by salmon and migratory cutthroat trout...well, we may have other saltwater fishing on our minds than the equatorial sort.

And we should—fly fishing along Pacific Northwest beaches can be remarkable. A couple of years ago it got even better here in Washington—new statewide regulations prohibited all killing of cutthroats caught in salt water. By the end of the first year of the new regs, I was hearing from anglers up and down Puget Sound and Hood Canal that cutthroat fishing was better than it had been in decades. The year after that? Use your imagination.

That doesn't mean it's necessarily easy even now to just go out and catch a sea-run cutthroat on the Washington coast. The "sea-run," as we often call him, moves to his own schedule and with his own motives, both of which are often a mystery to fly fishers. Only by studying his habits and spending considerable time learning specific areas he frequents will you catch him with any consistency. For starters, you'll need to fish areas protected from surf—trout seem to have no love of surf.

I don't mean to make this all sound too complex or intimidating—there are enough sea-runs along the coasts of Oregon, Washington, and British Columbia (Canada) that you'll always have a fair chance at catching some if you fish known cutthroat areas or just promising water. Which brings up the matter of recognizing promising sea-run water. It is, mainly, rocky areas (which often hold oysters—oyster beds are a welcome sight to the cutthroat angler); beds of long, fleshy, olive-brown blades of "eel grass"; and points of land, around which tidal currents flow. Finally, there are the stream-mouths and their brackish water where cutthroats often lurk. All these places may hold many, some, or no sea-runs at various stages of tide and at different seasons. Persistence is the only real way to catch sea-runs with any consistency—exploring new areas for them, and returning to familiar ones over various seasons, stages of tide, and times of day until you begin to understand how all the variables add up.

(Bear in mind, during your quest for cutthroats, that tidal currents and beaches varying from rock to soft muck require caution and common sense if you are to get about them safely. *Anyplace* out of doors comes with hazards, as so many fly fishers who fish rivers with rapids, slick rocks, and waterfalls know well.)

All said, this generally little-known form of fishing lies close at hand for millions of people living along the west coast of North America, and deserves a try from visiting anglers. Reason enough to investigate a few creative new flies designed for sea-run cutthroat trout.

Oyster beds—an excellent place to hunt sea-run cutthroat trout.

THE FLIES

The Jim Dandy is the creation of Jim Kerr, a guide on Washington's Olympic Peninsula. It's a sort of streamer that imitates various species of swimming saltwater worms upon which cutthroat feed. It's designed to sink in earnest—and it does—for versatility of depth on a full-floating or sink-tip line.

My own Raccoon is a general-purpose non-imitative sea-run fly. Simple and straightforward overall, its unusual dubbing and the way this material is applied are its only uncommon characteristics (though its tail is interesting)—but they apparently are attractive to sea-runs.

All the better sea-run anglers I know agree that their quarry is a great consumer of the "sculpin," a mottled-brown, broad-mouthed, flat-headed little fish that mostly lies on its belly on the bottom, making the occasional dart of startling precision and speed on the thrust of its enormous pectoral fins after some likely doomed prey. So I included Ron Bringle's sculpin-imitation, the Ron's Sculpin. Ron knows sea-runs—he spends much of his time either behind the counter at the Northwest Angler fly shop on Brainbridge Island, Washington helping other fly fishers figure out how to catch them or out chasing them himself around Puget Sound and Hood Canal.

All three of these flies catch not only sea-runs but salmon, too. I've seen feeding silver salmon come to the Jim Dandy. And

A sculpin.

I've caught scads of silvers, both feeding in open water and staging to spawn in estuaries, on the Raccoon—especially a Raccoon with a yellow body (though at times I've done better with a pink- or red-bodied Raccoon). Salmon feed on sculpin, just as sea-runs do, consequently a good many silver salmon have fallen for the Ron's Sculpin.

TYING TIPS

Since we'll soon tie the Jim Dandy step-by-step, I'll leave the finer points of creating that fly for the photos and captions to come. (The tying of my Raccoon is covered thoroughly in the next chapter, "The Raccoon.")

The two real challenges in tying the Ron's Sculpin are making the Matuka-style wing and forming the flared-hair head. Briefly put, patience, practice, and care are the only road to a good Matuka wing. And the same goes for flaring hair. If I could add only one point of advice regarding the hair, it would be that you use strong, heavy thread, even if you have to switch threads after the body and wing are formed. I use size-A—or even size-D—rod thread for all my flared-hair work. Finer thread will break before it can really compress down to flare the hair and lock it in place. One more point: Ron likes to really tighten the rib over the hackle-wing so the fibers stick up spine-like, as in the photo. Why? Because sculpins are spiny.

Two fine sea-run cutthroat trout, caught and released by the author and his friend Jeffery Delia in Washington State's Hood Canal.

RACCOON   *Skip Morris*

(Author's note: the Raccoon is fully explored in the chapter titled "The Raccoon." So why go through the details of that pattern again here? You'll find all you need to know about it beginning on page 98.)

RON'S SCULPIN   *Ron Bringle*

HOOK: Heavy wire, curved shank, size 6.

THREAD: Yellow 3/0, 6/0, or 8/0. (I prefer gray size-A or -D rod-winding thread for the head.)

RIB: Fine gold wire. (I perfer fine copper wire.)

BODY: Yellow, cream, orange, or gold floss.

WING: Two big cree or grizzly dry-fly rooster hackles.

HEAD: Natural-gray deer hair with a slim band of black or brown in the center.

JIM DANDY   *Jim Kerr*

HOOK: Heavy wire, 3X long, size 8 (Jim uses the Tiemco 5263).

HEAD: Gold cone head, 3/16th-inch.

THREAD: Six-ought in orange, yellow, or white.

WEIGHT: Lead or lead-substitute wire, 0.020 inch (or .025), one layer.

TAIL: Two to four strands of orange (or pearl) Flashabou inside very pale, creamy orange marabou (Jim dyes this color himself. The commercial color "apricot" is a good substitute). One plume normally, but use two if the plumes are skimpy.

RIB: Copper wire, medium.

BODY: Silver tinsel under light-orange floss.

COLLAR: Shiny pale-orange synthetic dubbing. (Jim uses Partridge's SLF dubbing in "Sunset Orange"; I use Arizona Sparkle Nymph Dubbing in "Skip's October Caddis.")

The author fishing along a beach in Washington State's Hood Canal for sea-run cutthroat trout—and catching them!

Carol Ann Morris

TYING THE JIM DANDY

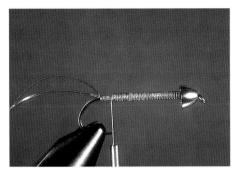

1. Slip the cone up the hook's shank to its eye. Mount the hook in your vise; then start the thread on the shank and wind it back to the hook's bend. Wind a layer of lead or lead-substitute wire from directly over the hook's point up the shank to the cone (leaving a little bare shank at the bend). Trim the ends of the lead wire.

Bind two to four strands of Flashabou at the bend, projecting back.

2. Snip off the butt of a full marabou plume, work the butt-fibers down around the shank behind the lead, and then bind the butts. (Use two plumes, if they are thin.) The tail should be long—1 1/2 to 2 times the shank's length.

You are trying to build up the shank to match the diameter of the lead, so make sure you bind the Flashabou and marabou right up against the rear of the lead windings.

3. Bind a length of medium-diameter copper wire along the shank to the bend. Trim off the front end of the wire, if necessary. Spiral the thread forward to the metal cone.

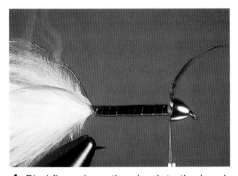

4. Bind floss down the shank to the bend. Spiral the thread forward to the cone; then bind flat silver tinsel along the shank to the bend. (If it is Mylar, two-color tinsel, bind it silver-side-down, so the silver side will show when you wrap the tinsel.) Trim off the stub-ends of the floss and tinsel. Wind the tinsel forward to the cone. Bind the end of the tinsel just behind the cone. Trim off the end of the tinsel.

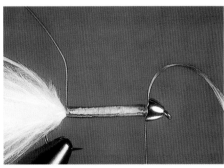

5. Wind the floss up the tinsel to the cone; bind the end of the floss with a few tight thread-turns, just behind the cone; and then trim off the end of the floss. Wind on only *one* layer of floss—so the tinsel will lightly shine through it when the fly is wet.

6. Wind the copper wire up the floss in four to six ribs. Bind the end of the wire just behind the cone; trim off the end of the wire.

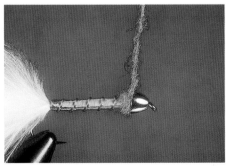

7. Spin dubbing onto the thread and dub a short, full collar at the rear of the cone. Whip finish the thread between the dubbing and cone, trim the end of the thread, and then work some head cement down to the whip finish. Jim Dandy completed.

THE RACCOON

BEAD:	Black, gold, copper, or silver in whatever size you like. (I prefer gold and black, 5/8" for size-8 and -6 hooks.)
HOOK:	Heavy wire, 1X long (standard nymph hook), sizes 12 to 6.
THREAD:	Three-ought, 6/0, or 8/0 in the body's color (white thread for a pink body).
TAIL:	Grizzly hen-neck hackle-fibers.
BODY:	Black, red, pink, or yellow dubbing (chartreuse, cream, and orange are under investigation). The dubbing is rabbit blended with Lite Brite or Angel Hair (fine Mylar strips) in silver, pearl, and a similar color to that of the rabbit. (Or Arizona Flyfishing's Sparkle Nymph Dubbing.)
HACKLE:	Undyed grizzly (regardless of body color) hen-neck hackle-fibers (Whiting's Soft Hackle is my favorite for large hooks).

Despite all the fan fare over cut-wing thises, extended-body thats, and other complicated fly designs, a great many fly fishers often fish Brassies, San Juan Worms, and other equally simple fly patterns. Always have. And, I've no doubt, always will.

They do so because many simple fly patterns work.

So I'd like to tell you about a particular simple fly that works. I designed it to billow with life at every twitch of the leader, to sink lazily, to glint in daylight—essentially, to capture the interest of the cutthroat trout in my local beaver ponds. Turned out it does this very well. Then I discovered that it also held a strong attraction for sea-run cutthroat trout in salt water, in the fresh water of the streams they ascend for their spawning, and in the brackish water of the estuaries they continually revisit.

Then we had a big year for silver salmon.

Hundreds of them slashed and darted nervously about the river and creek mouths, each fish waiting its turn to enter fresh water, spawn, and die. In the estuaries most were still bright and strong, but they were moody and sullen, too, and ignored a lot of flies—all the local fly fishers were finding that. But I was just fishing my plain little beaver-pond fly for sea-run cutts at a local creek mouth when I started hooking salmon. So I kept on fishing that fly and kept on hooking salmon—silvers up to thirteen pounds in three different creek mouths that September and October, lots of silvers.

When it was all about over for the year, I began to wonder if my fly had really been all that good. I mean, maybe on that first day it *was* that good, but perhaps after that the fish only hit it because they'd hit any fly. Then I fished a creek mouth with my friend Jeffrey Delia. Jeffrey's a fanatic for creek mouths, an oyster farmer (and photographer) who picks up a rod regularly throughout the fall and winter. We'd done well with the silvers, hooking a fish every ten minutes or so for two hours of a good tide, and back at the cars we chatted and compared flies. We both laughed with surprise when, dangling from tippets, side by side, our flies were nearly one in form, color, and size. Clearly, the salmon wanted a sparkly little wet fly.

Somewhere along the way, I tried adding a metal bead to a Raccoon and came to prefer the fly that way—the heavy bead pulls the fly right down and helps hold it there.

So my Raccoon had proved effective on sea-runs, and oddly so on staging silver salmon. But one test remained: would saltwater salmon in their feeding prime—not the dour non-feeding migrants roaming the estuaries—go for a Raccoon? In a nutshell, they did. In fact, it sometimes seemed to be the only fly they would take. Why would real feeding salmon ignore streamers that look like the candlefish and herring they eat daily yet clamp onto a red, bright little swimming thing completely unlike anything they've ever seen? I have no answers, no reasonable theories. But now when I know I'll be out casting to salmon in salt water, I make sure I have Raccoons on hand.

At the top, a typical fly for Pacific salmon; lower left, the Delia brothers' Squash; lower right, the Raccoon. Any two seem related? (Only the Raccoon was tied by the author.)

A fine silver salmon displaying the red Raccoon it took after refusing conventional streamer patterns.

THE DESIGN

My beaver-pond fly that has moved so many sea-runs and salmon (and, for that matter, beaver-pond cutthroat) is a wet fly, and an especially simple one: a tail, a body, a hackle (a bead at its head is optional); no rib, no tag, no wings—simply put, no frills. Back when I was just trying to work out a fly for the ponds, it had a silver-tinsel rib. But the tinsel turned out to be the weakest part of the fly, and I didn't like the effect anyway. That's when I started working on a dubbing that would do what I wanted done.

What I wanted was something brighter than that quiet sheen of many synthetic dubbings like Antron. I wanted the twinkles and little flashes you see from a back swimmer or a ready-to-emerge chironomid pupa. I had already worked out something close for my signature Skip Nymphs, for when I used them to imitate *Callibaetis* mayfly nymphs ripe to hatch in lakes, sparkling in their translucent, gas-filled shucks; it was a combination of Angel Hair or Lite Brite (in other words, fine Mylar strips) and squirrel or hare's mask fur, blended. So I mixed some of my dubbing in colors I'd learned that sea-runs like—pink, sunny yellow, red,

black—and tried them in my new fly. The pond trout went for it. Then the sea runs approved. It was yellow that caught that first silver salmon, and yellow that proved to be the best choice for salmon in all the creek mouths that fall. Jeffrey assures me that in other years he's done well on silvers with his close cousin to the Raccoon (the Squash, developed by Jeffery and his brother Russell) with a body in pink, in white, or gray.

The makeup of the dubbing is not, I believe, the only factor behind the effectiveness of the Raccoon; equally important is *how* the dubbing is applied—long and shaggy, in a dubbing loop—and, to a lesser degree, the soft, lively fibers in the tail. I expected the hackle collar to be the real performer in this fly, but after shooting a segment of the "Fly Fish TV" show and later seeing the Raccoon shot close up with an underwater camera, it was plain that the long sparkling body-fibers and fluffy tail did most of the dancing.

(Note: I use a standard nymph hook in my Raccoons. If you do the same, be sure to rinse it thoroughly in fresh water after it's been fished in the salt.)

DETAILS ON THE DUBBING

An otherwise conventional fly, the Raccoon has three unusual features: its dubbing, the shagginess of that dubbing in the fly's body, and the particular sort of hackle fibers that make up its tail. We'll look at the tail and *how* to dub the body later. Here we'll look at how to make the dubbing.

I add three colors of chopped Mylar to rabbit fur: a color similar to the color of the fur, silver, and pearl (or clear). The colors should be of about equal amounts. So yellow fur, for example, would be blended with yellow, silver, and pearl Mylar. It's hard to describe the ratio of fur to Mylar, but this should explain it adequately: when a fly containing this dubbing is turned under light, it should show *obvious* sparkle—nothing subtle. But that doesn't

take a whole lot of Mylar. Use the photos as a guide. I usually cut the Mylar to about 3/8-inch lengths, but that will vary a lot, which is good. I hand-blend the fur and Mylar, as described in the captions to come.

There is now a simpler way to get the dubbing for a Raccoon, and I believe it's a better way—go to your local fly shop and pick up some Sparkle Nymph Dubbing. Arizona Flyfishing, Inc. makes this improved version of my original; it's a spiky blend that includes fine wool to hold everything together. The colors I use in my Raccoon are, by the company's names, Black, Skip's Red, Skip's Soft Yellow, and Skip's Pink.

VARIATIONS and SIZES

I fish Raccoons with bead heads more often than Raccoons without. The heavy bead helps carry the fly down a bit, and gives it a lively dip-and-rise action on a retrieve, which sea-run cutts and salmon find most appealing. For the subtle approach, I use a Raccoon without a bead—it's especially good in small beaver ponds, where the fly sinks slowly and gives an enticing little quiver of its tail, body, and collar with even the slightest tug on the line. For beaver ponds I like it best with a black body on hooks of size 12 and 10, and so, it seems, do the trout.

For sea-run cutthroat I usually end up using Raccoons in sizes 10, 8, and, if the fish are running large, 6. Colors for cutthroats, in my order of preference, are yellow, pink, red, and black.

For salmon feeding in open water, sizes 8 and 6. Red and yellow seem most consistently productive, but pink and black can be just as good.

For salmon staging in the stream mouths, sizes 8 and 6—small as that may seem for salmon up to ten pounds and heavier—get the strikes. Yellow is clearly the most dependable, with pink and red ocassionally best.

As you can see, a size-8 yellow raccoon is always a promising choice along salmon and cutthroat beaches.

Carol Ann Morris

1. Here's how to make the dubbing for the Raccoon. Spread out a bunch of loose rabbit fur until it is fairly flat, and then lay it on a flat surface. From wads of fine Mylar strips, snip short bunches off the ends onto the rabbit, one color at a time—use three colors of Mylar, as previously described under "Details on the Dubbing."

2. Fold the fur over the Mylar, and then pull the fur bunch in half. Pinch the two halves together and pull them apart again. Continue repeating this sequence until the fur and Mylar are blended.

3. Here's how the completed dubbing should look—well-blended, mostly fur but with enough Mylar to add obvious sparkle.

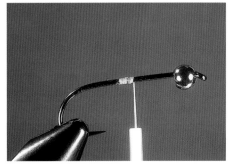

4. Slip a bead, small end of the hole first, over the hook's point and then slide it up to the hook's eye (if you plan to include a bead, that is). Mount the hook in your vise. Start the thread at about the middle of the hook's shank. Strip a full bunch of fibers off the side of a hen-neck hackle.

5. The best tail fibers, I find, come from the lower-center of a wide, webby hen hackle—the same hackle, in fact, that I use later for the hackle collar. The trick is to use mostly the fibers between the firm and the fluffy—the transitional fibers separating the two extremes. (Though it doesn't hurt to include a few of the lower downy fibers.)

6. Combine the tailing fibers you removed from both sides of the hackle; then bind the resulting bunch atop the shank (back to the hook's bend) so that they project off the bend a distance about equal to the shank's length or, at most, the full hook's length.

7. Pull out the bobbin to expose about a foot and a half of thread. Wax the thread; then double it back to the hook. Add a few thread-turns back over the base of the thread-loop you just formed—these last turns will secure the base of the loop. Spiral the working-thread up most of the shank.

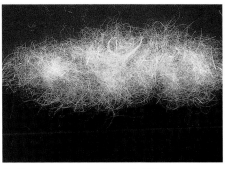

8. Tease a bunch of the dubbing out into a sort of broad, flat strip as shown. Lay the strip on a flat surface.

If the strip of dubbing is too wide, no problem. Once the fly is completed, you can lightly tug off any dubbing that wasn't caught in the loop, and then use it in the next Raccoon.

9. Pick up the dubbing-strip along its edge in a big bulldog clip. (These are available in office supply stores, and cheap. Mine is three inches across.) I picked this dubbing-loop method up from a Swedish fly tier named Robert Lai.

10. Hold open the dubbing loop and insert the dubbing-strip lengthwise, in line with the loop. Pinch the sides of the loop together to hold the dubbing; then twist the loop with a dubbing whirl or dubbing twister until everything gathers into a sort of furry rope.

11. Wind this dubbing-rope up the shank in close, tight turns. (It helps to stroke back the dubbing before winding on each turn.) Continue winding the dubbing loop until it lies firmly up against the bead, to fill the large hole in the back of the bead (or, without a bead, dub to just short of the hook's eye).

You can dub in conventional fashion, but if you do, dub very heavily and really pick out the fibers afterwards.

12. Secure the end of the rope under tight thread-turns, and then trim off its end. Using your hackle gauge, find a barred (grizzly) *hen neck* hackle one size too large (two sizes at most) for your hook. Bind the hackle by its bare stem just behind the bead (or with no bead, just behind the eye), wind the thread back to the front of the body, and trim off the hackle's stem.

13. Wind the hackle back to the body in three or four close turns. Wind a turn or two of thread over the hackle's tip, and then spiral the thread *forward* through the hackle to the bead (or the hook's eye, if there is no bead). This method crosses the hackle's stem with turns of thread for a tough hackle collar.

14. Find and trim out the hackle's tip. Stroke back and then hold the hackle's fibers as you build a thread collar behind the bead (or a tapered thread head, if you omitted the bead). Coat the collar (or thread head) with head cement to complete the Raccoon.

15. Take a close look at the bead; it may be out of alignment when viewed either from the side or top. If it is off, and that bothers you (it won't bother the fish), you can easily align the bead. Just grip it in pliers and adjust it firmly. Don't get too aggressive—you *could* break the hook. Smooth-jawed pliers will scar the bead least, but then so what if the bead shows a scratch or two?

I've always felt that you, the reader, and I have a tacit understanding: You read what I write, and I tell you the truth to the best of my ability, even if that means occasionally admitting how little I know about my subject. Therefore I confess that on the matter of flies for summer-run steelhead I'm no authority. (I did, however, tie commercially a few hundred steelhead flies during my early years in the fly-fishing business. But it takes a lot more than that to make a real steelheader.) So I turned to my friend Troy Dettman, owner of the North West Angler fly shop in Winslow, Washington, for help. Much of what follows came from him.

LIGHT AND DARK

The broadest way steelhead fly fishers see their flies is as overall dark or light. But most steelhead flies are, in fact, a bit of both—for example, even the Skunk, a really dark fly, with it's black body, black tail, and black hackle, has a white wing. A good many steelhead flies would be hard to categorize either way, being blends of bright colors, mixed colors or hues (such as natural and dyed barred hackle with its pale and black stripes), and other colors somewhere between dark and light—is bright medium-blue, for example, a light color or a dark one?

Yes, there are other important considerations in deciding which steelhead fly is right for the moment—hook size, fullness of dressing, hook weight, and more. But with most steelhead fly fishers, the question of light or dark probably comes first. And even if light and dark is a difficult idea to pin down with specifics, it remains that a good steelhead fly fisher will judge the overall hue of each fly and fish it according to his view of when and how light and dark flies should be fished.

Troy's four favorite light and dark flies for summer steelhead reflect the murkiness of the light-and-dark concept, and beyond that are probably even more peculiar than what most experienced steelheaders would choose—such as a fly called *Winter's* Hope for *summer* steelhead? But bear in mind that Troy owns a fly shop, guides fly fishers for summer-run steelhead, and fishes for these anadromous rainbow trout (currently classified as salmon, but tomorrow? who knows) all over the Pacific Northwest. His opinions carry the weight of experience.

Above is a collection of steelhead flies ranging from the standard to the obscure. Which ones would you consider dark, and which light? I find three of them tough to call.

LIGHT

Troy's first choice for an all-around light-color summer-steelhead fly is Bill McMillan's Winter's Hope. As it's name implies, it was indeed designed for winter fish and is normally tied on the big hooks of that season, hooks of size 1/0 up to 6/0. But Troy has found the Winter's Hope consistently effective on summer fish when tied on smaller hooks of size 6 to 2. More than anything else it is a *bright* fly. Though a light one as well.

The second of Troy's light summer-run flies—the Lady Caroline—was born long ago in Scotland and has been altered considerably since its arrival in North America. If there were a category for flies right in between light and dark, the Lady Caroline would hover very near it. But when a light fly is called for, Troy often shows the fish a Lady Caroline, and it often produces. This fly is at its best in late summer and fall, when the October Caddis is active. Many fish move to it convinced, Troy believes, they have found another rising pupa of the great caddis.

Here are Winter's Hopes tied for both winter and summer steelhead—impressive range of hook sizes, eh?

DARK

For a day-in, day-out dark summer-steelhead fly, Troy relies on the ever-popular Purple Peril. His favorite way to fish it is as a follow-up fly; it works like this: Troy begins with a waking surface fly, such as a Muddler Minnow, and right after a fish moves to it but fails to actually take it, Troy switches to the Purple Peril and drifts it through with the greased-line method. In ninety percent of such cases, he says, the steelhead takes solid hold of the second, slightly deeper fly.

Troy's own fly, the Ketchum, is his second choice for a dark summer-run fly. It's a sort of spey fly with hackle shorter than usual. He ties it, as you'll see, with most of its components always in black, and always with matching butt and wing in one of three bright colors.

CONSIDERATIONS

All of Troy's choices are subsurface flies, the sort that are fished on the steelheader's version of the wet-fly swing or by the greased-line method. And all lack the metal eyes of the Comets and the lead-barbell eyes of some of the newer quick-sinking flies, so that while the Winter's Hope and Lady Caroline and the rest of Troy's four do sink, they do so in leisurely fashion.

Then there's fly size—it's a whole different ball game with summer-run steelhead when compared with winter fish. For summer-runs, Troy usually fishes flies on hooks from size 6 to 2.

When a river is still high from runoff or rain in early summer, he always fishes flies on the big end of that range—and if the water is colored, big *dark* flies. For low water, he prefers flies on the smaller hooks, size 6, and perhaps 4. Generally, he says, the lower the water, the smaller the fly.

When to use light and when to use dark flies for summer-runs? Troy says that in the low light of early morning and sunset he fishes dark flies, leaving light flies for the brighter, middle part of the day. And, as I mentioned, dark flies always for high or colored water.

Try a light fly if the water is low to modest height, especially in the bright middle part of the day.

Try a dark fly if the water is high (especially if it's high and colored), and during the low light of sunrise and sunset.

THE FOLDED HACKLE

Though other kinds of fly patterns can or should take a folded hackle, it is most common on flies for steelhead and Atlantic salmon. Therefore, a piece on flies for summer-run steelhead is certainly a logical place for exploring the folded hackle and the tying techniques it requires.

I'll show you an easy alternative to the folded hackle. It involves winding the hackle *back* to the front of the body (not the usual direction) and then toughening it by spiraling the thread *forward* through the turns of hackle; the hackle gets its folded effect just by pinching its fibers down, which works surprisingly well.

When this is done, I'll show you a more traditional method for creating a folded hackle. The time and care required to create a true folded hackle are, to many tiers, justified by the results.

WINTER'S HOPE   *Bill McMillan*

HOOK: Heavy wire steelhead-Atlantic salmon, sizes 6 to 2 (for summer fish).
THREAD: Claret 6/0.
BODY: Flat silver tinsel.
WING: Two yellow hackle tips inside two orange hackle tips.
TOPPING: A small bunch of light-olive calf tail.
HACKLE: A few turns of purple hackle in front of a few turns of turquoise.

LADY CAROLINE

HOOK: Heavy wire steelhead-Atlantic salmon, or low-water hook, sizes 6 to 2.
THREAD: Black or claret 6/0.
TAIL: Golden pheasant breast-feather fibers.
RIB: Fine oval gold or silver tinsel.
BODY: Blended seal-fur substitute, one part olive, two parts light brown.
THROAT: Golden pheasant breast-feather fibers.
WING: Bronze mallard.
COMMENTS: The Lady Caroline is normally tied in "low-water" style, dressed lightly and tied noticeably short on the hook. Troy always ties it in low-water style.

PURPLE PERIL   *Ken Mcleod*

HOOK: Heavy wire steelhead-Atlantic salmon hook, sizes 6 to 2.
THREAD: Black 6/0.
WING: Brown buck tail.
TAIL: Purple hackle-fibers.
RIB: Flat or oval silver tinsel.
BODY: Purple chenille.
HACKLE: Purple.

KETCHUM   *Troy Dettman*

HOOK: Heavy wire, steelhead-Atlantic salmon, sizes 6 to 2.
THREAD: Black 6/0.
BODY: Rear third: floss in hot pink, red, or chartreuse, over flat gold tinsel. Front two thirds: black dubbing (any bright dubbing, such as SLF or Scintilla, that is long fibered enough to pick out).
RIB: Oval gold tinsel.
HACKLE: Black schlappen, tied in by its tip, palmered over the front two-thirds of the body, alongside the rib, and then wound in a few close turns just behind the hook's eye. The fibers should be somewhat shorter than usual for a spey fly.
WING: Calf tail dyed hot pink, red, or chartreuse (the wing should be the color of the floss), sparse and slightly short.

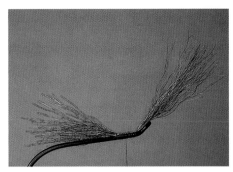

1. Tying the Purple Peril. Start the thread at the hook's eye. Bind some stacked brown buck tail atop the hook's shank at the eye. The buck tail, folded back, should reach the far edge of the hook's bend.

2. Spiral the thread back to the hook's bend. Bind on the tail fibers there. The length of the tail should about equal the hook's gape.

3. Bind some oval or flat silver tinsel, then some chenille, from the bend forward up the shank to just a little back from the eye.

4. Wind the chenille forward to just back from the eye, bind its end with tight thread-turns, trim it. Wind the tinsel forward in four to six ribs, bind its end at the front of the body, and trim it closely.

5. Strip the fluffy fibers from the base of a big saddle hackle. Bind the hackle by its stem a little *forward* of the body, trim the stem, and then wind the thread *back* to the front of the body. Note where the hackle is bound and where the thread hangs in the photograph.

6. Wind the hackle *back* to the body in a few close turns. Spiral the thread *forward* through the hackle in a few tight turns. Trim off the hackle's tip.

The hackle fibers should now cant back a little. And the stem is reinforced by the turns of thread that cross it.

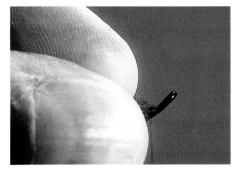

7. Fold the wing back. Pinch the hackle down hard all around its base. Stroke wing and hackles back, and then build a small thread head.

8. Here's the completed wing and pinched-down hackle. Whip finish the thread, trim it, and cement the head.

Next, a real folded hackle.

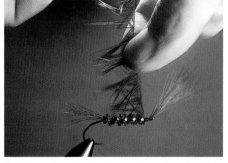

9. Bind a hackle by its tip at the front of the body. Trim off the tip. Stroke the fibers out from the stem, and then stroke them back, so that all fibers are behind the stem. Pinch the fibers at their bases—pinch hard, so they stay back.

10. Wind the hackle forward in close turns. With each turn, stroke back the fibers so that they lie neatly, canted rearward.

11. Here is what a real folded hackle looks like. Note that the fibers all slant steeply back and are even and neat.

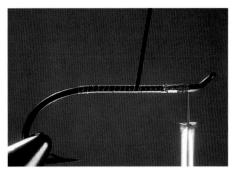

1. Here's how to tie the Winter's Hope. Start the thread just back from the hook's eye. Bind on some flat Mylar tinsel, silver side up. Wind the tinsel in close turns back to the hook's bend, then back up to where it started. Bind the end of the tinsel, then trim it off.

2. Trim two yellow and two orange hackle tips to one length; they should about equal the full length of the hook, but can be *slightly* longer.

3. Bind the yellow pair of hackles, cupped together, atop the shank just back from the eye.

4. Bind the orange hackles outside the yellow, cupped together (or just bind on all four at once). There shouldn't be anything to trim, but if the hackles' butts protrude too far, trim them.

I didn't strip the fibers from the bases of these hackles—the hackles tend to stay in position best this way, I find. But you can strip their very points if you prefer.

5. Comb, then stack a small bunch of calf tail. Bind the bunch just ahead of the wing. Trim and bind the butts of the hair, if necessary.

6. Find a blue saddle hackle whose fibers are slightly longer than the shank. Strip the fibers from the base of the hackle's stem. Bind the hackle by its tip (or butt); then trim off the tip (or butt). Advance the thread a little, wind the hackle forward in just a few turns, and then bind the hackle's butt (or tip). (You can, of course, fold the hackle.)

7. Prepare, bind on, wrap, and trim a purple saddle hackle in front of the blue hackle, just as you did the blue hackle. Create and complete the usual thread head.

THE EGG-SUCKING LEECH

HOOK:	Heavy wire, 3X or 4X long, size 2 or 4.
THREAD:	Black 6/0 or 3/0. (Or a color to blend with the body.)
WEIGHT (optional):	Lead or lead-substitute wire, under the body.
TAIL:	Purple marabou for a purple fly, black for a black fly.
HACKLE:	Purple saddle hackle (black for a black fly).
BODY:	Purple chenille for a purple fly (black for a black fly).
HEAD:	Fluorescent-pink or -red chenille.

How many fly fishers *don't* dream of Alaska? Not many, I'll wager.

The magnificence of Alaska is certainly the stuff of dreams. It's a gargantuan state—over twice the size of the second biggest American state, massive Texas—but with only about half the population of the smallest state, tiny Rhode Island. (Just how tiny *is* Rhode Island?: 1,212 square miles. Alaska: about 1,212 square miles X 488). Few people, vast land. Alaska's tidal shoreline is estimated, on average, at about 40,000 miles, meaning that if it were straightened it could circle the Earth roughly one and a half times. From that shoreline the land rises into several mountain ranges, which include the highest peak in North America (Mount McKinley). The Alaskan winter of '71, in someplace called Prospect Creek, missed eighty degrees Fahrenheit below zero by only two tenths of a degree. The summer of 1915, however, pushed tiny Fort Yukon's temperature to 100 above. I could go one with such staggering statistics, but you get the idea.

It is country in whose presence we humans feel like the tiniest of spiders—fragile, frightened, and perilously under foot. The sheer magnitude of its primitive splendor inspires our imaginations.

So, imagine how many fish there are in Alaska.

A lot, I'll wager.

There were certainly a lot of fish the last time I went looking for them in Alaska. In one week I caught at least a hundred and fifty silver salmon from sixteen to twenty pounds, a few dozen Dolly Varden from ten inches to two-and-a-half pounds, one brutish and mottled chum salmon, two snaky spawned-out steelhead, and a ten-inch rainbow trout.

Most of those salmon came to an Egg-Sucking Leech—an absolutely standard fly pattern for Alaska salmon. (Though I actually used a variation, called the Egg-Sucking Bunny Leech, with a body and tail of rabbit fur instead of the usual chenille and hackle.)

So the next time you picture yourself fishing in Alaska, you probably need to work a black or purple Egg-Sucking Leech into the scene.

It's an odd fly: a fluffy tail and a thick, spiky body, all in black or unnatural purple, with a bright fuzzy ball for a head. Even its name is odd, if not offensive. ("Egg-Sucking Leech"—how'd you like being called *that*?) But it works, as consistently as any fly works on impulsive salmon, and I doubt many seasoned Alaska fly fishers go to a river or estuary without a few on hand.

Brian O'Keefe

EGG-SUCKING BUNNY LEECH

HOOK:	Same style and sizes as for the standard Egg-Sucking Leech.
WEIGHT (optional):	Lead or lead-substitute wire.
THREAD:	Six-ought or 3/0 in the body's color.
TAIL:	A black or purple Zonker strip.
BODY:	Black or purple crosscut-rabbit strip.
HEAD:	Fluorescent-pink or -red chenille.

Created by Alaskan Will Bauer, the Egg-Sucking Leech is effective for all the salmons, and for steelhead, rainbow trout, and Dolly Varden char. But it's not just an Alaska fly; it's popular throughout the Pacific Northwest and in the Great Lakes Region of the northeastern United States.

Fishing an Egg-Sucking Leech has always seemed pretty straightforward to me: Toss the fly out among the fish (salmon are often in plain sight), and then tease it back at whatever speed and in whatever way triggers a strike. Usually, I've found, this means a jerky retrieve of moderate speed, with occasional pauses.

The name "Egg-Sucking Leech" is no anomaly, but part of a long and noble tradition of distasteful fly titles. In the company of the Cowdung, Booby Nymph, and Moose Turd, "Egg-Sucking Leech" rings almost poetic.

TYING THE STANDARD EGG-SUCKING LEECH

1. Start the thread well up the hook's shank. Bind a whole marabou plume along the top of the shank to the hook's bend (no closer than 1/8 inch to the hook's eye). The resulting marabou tail should be at least as long as the shank, but no longer than the full length of the hook.

2. Trim off the butt of the plume. Bind a hackle an inch or so up from its tip (where the stem is strong) at the bend. (You can strip the long, fluffy fibers from the butt of the hackle, and then bind the hackle by its stripped stem, if you prefer.)

3. Bind a length of chenille from behind the eye to the bend. Trim off the short, forward end of the chenille. Spiral the thread about three quarters of the way up the shank. Wind the chenille in close turns up the shank to the hanging thread.

4. Bind the end of the chenille and then trim it off. Wind the hackle by its butt in four to seven turns up the chenille body. Bind the end of the hackle and trim it off.

5. Bind the end of some fluorescent chenille at the front of the body. Trim off the stub-end of the chenille. Advance the thread to just behind the eye. Wind the chenille back and forth in two or more layers to build a fuzzy ball.

6. Bind the end of the chenille just behind the eye. Trim off the stub-end of the chenille. Build a small tapered thread head, whip finish the thread, and cut the thread. Complete the Egg-Sucking Leech by coating the thread head with head cement.

TYING THE EGG-SUCKING BUNNY LEECH

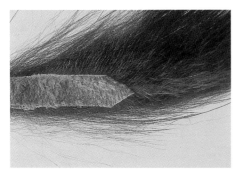

1. Trim a point on the end of a "Zonker strip," a strip of rabbit hide with the fur sloping along the length of the strip. The point should be cut from the *hide only*— not the fur—and cut from the end towards which the fur slopes.

2. Start the thread just ahead of the hook's bend. Bind the pointed Zonker strip atop the hook's shank, at the bend. The resulting tail (measured by the hide strip, not the fur) should be about two thirds the length of the shank (though tail-length on this fly is pretty subjective). Trim off the upper end of the strip.

3. Now you need a strip of "crosscut rabbit," a fur-and-hide strip like a Zonker strip, but with the fur sloping off to the *side*. Bind the the strip, by only about 1/4 inch or so of its end, so that when you wrap it forward, the fur will slope back, towards the tail, not forward.

4. Advance the thread about three quarters up the shank. Wind the strip in consecutive turns to the hanging thread. Bind the end of the strip, and then trim it off.

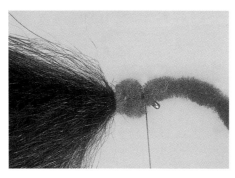

5. Bind down the end of some fluorescent-pink or -red chenille at the front of the body. Trim the end of the chenille. Build and complete the egg-head, then a thread head, as previously described for the standard Egg-Sucking Leech.

6. If you leave off the egg-head, you wind up with the "Bunny Leech," a general leech-imitation for trout, largemouth bass, smallmouth bass, and about any fish that'll eat a leech. Typical colors for leech patterns include black, brown, green, tan, olive, and, yes, purple.

THE ARTICLES in MORRIS ON TYING FLIES

ARTICLE TITLE PAGE #	COLUMN	MAGAZINE	DATE
"The King's River Caddis" Page 7	"Skip's Tying Bench"	*Salmon Trout Steelheader*	April-May 1998
"The Midge" Page 8	"Skip's Tying Bench"	*Salmon Trout Steelheader*	October-November 1997
"The Madam X" Page 9	"Foundation Flies"	*Fly Tyer*	Summer 1996
"The Gulper Special" Page 11	"Skip's Tying Bench"	*Salmon Trout Steelheader*	August-September 1998
"The Ant Carol" Page 13	"Northwest Fly Tying" (section)	*Northwest Fly Fishing*	Fall 1999
"Standard Variations on Standard Dry Flies" Page 15	"Morris on Tying"	*Flyfishing & Tying Journal*	Summer 1999
"The Bi-Visible" Page 18	"Skip's Tying Bench"	*Salmon Trout Steelheader*	June-July 1999
"The Fluttering Salmon Fly (or the F-150)" Page 19	"Morris on Tying"	*Flyfishing & Tying Journal*	Spring 2003
"The Royal Coachman and Lime Coachman Trudes" Page 21 (appeared as "The Royal Coachman Trude")	"Foundation Flies"	*Fly Tyer*	Autumn 1997
"The Tom Thumb" Page 23	feature article	*Fly Tyer*	Summer 2001
"The Chernobyl Ant" Page 25	"Foundation Flies"	*Fly Tyer*	Summer 1999
"The Feather Duster" Page 28	"Skip's Tying Bench"	*Salmon Trout Steelheader*	June-July 1997
"The Zebra Midge" Page 29	"Skip's Tying Bench"	*Salmon Trout Steelheader*	December-January 1997
"Bird's Stonefly Nymph" Page 30	"Foundation Flies"	*Fly Tyer*	Spring 1996
"The Halfback" Page 32	"Skip's Tying Bench"	*Salmon Trout Steelheader*	December-January 1998
"The Gray Nymph" Page 33	"Skip's Tying Bench	*Salmon Trout Steelheader*	February-March 1999
"The Royal Flush" Page 34	"Morris on Tying"	*Flyfishing & Tying Journal*	Spring 2005
"The Montana Stone" Page 37	"Foundation Flies"	*Fly Tyer*	Autumn/Winter 1996
"Egg Flies" Page 38	"Morris on Tying"	*Flyfishing & Tying Journal*	Winter 2001
"The Green Damsel" Page 42	"Foundation Flies"	*Fly Tyer*	Summer 1998
"Scud Flies" Page 44 (appeared as "Scuds")	"Morris on Tying"	*Flyfishing & Tying Journal*	Fall 2000
"The Foam PMD Emerger" Page 48	"Skip's Tying Bench"	*Salmon Trout Steelheader*	June-July 1998
"The Dark Cahill Wet Fly" Page 49	"Skip's Tying Bench"	*Salmon Trout Steelheader*	December-January 1999
"Soft-Hackled Flies" Page 50	"Morris on Tying"	*Flyfishing & Tying Journal*	Spring 2002
"The Partridge Caddis Emerger" Page 53	"Morris on Tying"	*Flyfishing & Tying Journal*	Summer 2003
"Tying Tiny for Fall Trout" Page 55	"Morris on Tying"	*Flyfishing & Tying Journal*	Fall 1999
"Kamloops Stillwater Standards" Page 58	feature article	*Fly Tyer*	Winter 1998
"Three Flies for the Great Western Caddis" Page 63	feature article	*Flyfishing & Tying Journal*	Fall 2004
"The Peacock Chenille Leech" Page 69	"Skip's Tying Bench"	*Salmon Trout Steelheader*	
"The Half and Half" Page 70	"Morris on Tying"	*"Flyfishing & Tying Journal*	Summer 2004
"Streamers & Bucktails for Spring Streams" Page 73	"Morris on Tying"	*Flyfishing & Tying Journal*	Spring 2000
"The Lefty's Deceiver" Page 77 (appeared as "Lefty's Deceiver")	"Foundation Flies"	*Fly Tyer*	Autumn 1998
"The Zonker in General, and a Variation in Particular" Page 79 (appeared as "Tying the Zonker in General, and a Variation in Particular")	feature article	*Fly Tying*	Fall 1998
"Tap's Bug" Page 83	"Foundation Flies"	*Fly Tyer*	Winter 1998
"The Silver Outcast" Page 85	"Foundation Flies"	*Fly Tyer*	Summer 1997
"The McGinty Page 87	"Foundation Flies"	*Fly Tyer*	Winter 1997
"The Bomber and the Green Machine" Page 90	"Morris on Tying"	*Flyfishing & Tying Journal*	Fall 2002
"Three New Flies for Sea-Runs" Page 94 (appeared as "A Few New Flies for Sea-Runs")	"Morris on Tying"	*Flyfishing & Tying Journal*	Summer 2002
"The Raccoon" Page 98	feature article	*Fly Tyer*	Spring 2002
"Light and Dark Flies for Summer Steelhead" Page 102	"Morris on Tying"	*Flyfishing & Tying Journal*	Spring 2001
"The Egg-Sucking Leech" Page 107	"Foundation Flies"	*Fly Tyer*	Spring 1998

INDEX

Adams dry fly, 15
Adams Midge, 8
Allen, Farrow, 83, 85, 87
Ameletus mayfly, 34
ant, flying, 13
Ant Carol, 13-14
Arbona, Fred, 44
Atlantic Salmon Flies & Fishing, 90
attractor fly patterns, definition of, 34

back swmmer, 23
Baetis (blue-winged olive)
    mayfly, 8, 48, 55
Baetis Soft Hackle, 56, 57
Bailey, Dan, 85
Baltz, Tom, 55
bass bug, 9, 83
Bassin' with a Fly Rod, 83
Bates, Jr., Joseph, 90
Bauer, Will, 108
Befus, Brad, 44, 45
beetle, 55
Belows, Chris, 70
binocular magnifier, 56
Bi-Visible, 18
Big Hole River, 19, 53
Bighorn Shrimp, 44, 46
Bird, Cal, 30
Bird's Stonefly, dry, 30
Bird's Stonefly Nymph, 30-31
Black Ant (fly), 55, 56
Black Bass & the Fly Rod, 85
Black Mamba dry fly, 25
black-nose dace (fish), 73
Black-Nose Dace (fly), 73, 74, 75
Black Wulff, 39
Blue Dun dry fly, 15-17
    Thorax, 15-17
    Parachute, 15, 17
Booby Nymph, 108
Book of Fly Patterns, The, 77, 90
Bomber, 90-93
Bow River, 19
Brassie, 55, 56, 98
Brick Back Caddis (October Caddis),
    63, 64, 65, 66-67
    fishing, 64
Bringle, Ron, 95, 96
Brooks, Joe, 73
Bumble McDougal, 87
Bunny Leech, 109
Byford, Dan, 79

caddisfly, 7, 23, 53, 55, 59, 61, 63, 64, 65
    Hydropsyche, 55

October caddis, 55, 63-65, 103
    Rhyocophilla, 55
Cahill, Dan, 49
Cahill dry flies, 15, 49
Callibaetis mayfly, 99
candlefish, 98
Carey, Colonel, 59, 60
Carey Special, 59, 60, 62
Chan, Brian, 23, 26, 58, 59, 69
Chan, Carlyn, 26
Chernobyl Ant, 25-26
chironomid, 8, 45, 60
    fishing imitations of, 29, 60
    pupa, 29, 60
Cinnamon Ant (fly), 55, 56
Clouser, Bob, 70
Clouser Minnow, 70
Comet (fly), 103
Comparadun, 44
Complete Book of Western Hatches, 42
Cowdung (fly), 108
    cutthroat trout, sea-run, finding in
    salt water, 94

damselflies, 42, 43
Dark Cahill wet fly, 49
deer hair, vs. elk hair, 23, 65
Delia, Jeffery, 95, 98, 99
Delia, Russell, 99
Demchuck, Bill, 25-26
Dennis, Jack, 25, 74
Deschutes Cased Caddis, 63, 64
    fishing, 64
Deschutes River, 19, 63, 64
Dettman, Troy, 102, 103, 104
Doc Spratley, 60
dragonflies, 44, 49

Edson Tiger, (Dark and Light), 74, 75
Edson, William, 75
egg fly patterns, 38-41
    fishing, 39
    hooks for, 40
Egg-Sucking Bunny Leech, 107, 109
Egg-Sucking Leech, 107-108
elk hair, vs. deer hair, 23, 65
Elk Hair Caddis, 11
Ellis, Jack, 83, 87
Epoxy Scud, 44, 45

Feather Duster nymph, 28
Field and Stream, 83
Flick, Art, 73, 74
flies, tiny, 55-57
    tools for, 56

Flies for Trout, 87
Flies for Bass & Panfish, 83, 85
Fluttering Salmon Fly (F150), 19-20
"Fly Fish TV," 99
Fly Patterns of British Columbia, 23, 59
Fly Patterns of Yellowstone, 28
folded hackle, 104, 105
Foam PMD Emerger, 48
Fujii, Ken, 29
Fullback, 32

Gapen, Don, 74
'Gillie, The', 59, 60, 61
glasses, reading, 56
Glo-Bug, 39, 40, 41
Gray Nymph, 33
Griffith, George, 56
Griffith's Gnat, 55, 56
Green Damsel nymph, 42-43
Green Machine, 90, 91, 93
Green River (Wyoming), 19
Gulper Special, 11-12

Hafele, Rick, 42, 56, 64
Haig-Brown, Roderick, 59
Half and Half, 70-72
    colors for, 70
    fishing, 71
    lines for fishing, 71
    species for, 70
Halfback, 32, 59
Hazel, John, 64
Hellekson, Terry, 30, 42, 87
Helvie, Kent, 90
Henrys Fork of the Snake River, 53
herring, 98
Honey, Gordon, 59, 61
Hood Canal, 94, 95, 96
Hughes, Dave, 42
Hydropsyche caddisfly, 55

Illiamna Pinkie, 39, 40

Jacklyn, Bob, 19
Jacklyn's Giant Salmon Fly, 19
Jim Dandy, 95, 96, 97
Juracek, John, 28, 56

Kamloops, 59
Kamloops Lakes, Canada, 58, 59, 60, 61
Kerr, Jim, 39, 95, 96
Ketchum, 103, 104
King's River, California, 7
King's River Caddis, 7
Kreh, Lefty, 70, 77

Krystal Egg, 39, 40

Lac Le Jeune, Canada, 60
Lady Caroline, 103, 104
Lawson, Mike, 53
leech, 44, 69
Leeson, Ted, 39, 40
Lefty's Deceiver, 70, 77-78
Leighton Lake, Canada, 60
Leisenring, James, 42
Leiser, Eric, 77, 90, 91
Letort Spring Run, 55
Light Cahill wet fly, 49
Lindgren, Arthur, 23, 59, 60, 61
lines, fly, 45
    for Half and Half, 71
    sinking, 45
Lucas, Jason, 87
Lucas on Bass Fishing, 87
Lynch, Gene, 56

Madam X, 9-10
Madison River, 19
magnification, for tying flies, 56
Marinaro, Vincent, 16
Mathews, Craig, 28, 48, 56
materials, for tiny flies, 56
mayfly, 8, 11, 23, 39, 44, 48, 55, 99
    Baetis (blue-winged olive), 8, 48, 55
    Callibaetis, 99
    pale morning dun (PMD), 39, 48
    Tricorythodes, 55
    western March brown, 55
McGinty, 87-88
Mcleod, Ken, 104
McMillan, Bill, 103, 104
midge (chironomid), 8, 55, 60
    definitions of, 8
Midge (fly), 8
    Adams, 8
    Black, 8
    definitions of, 8
midge head, 56
Mikulak, Art, 61
Mikulak Sedge, 61, 63
    fishing, 64, 65
Miramichi River, 90, 93
Missouri, upper, 53
Montana Stone, 37
Montanabou, 37
Mormon cricket, 25
Morris & Chan on Fly Fishing Trout
    Lakes, 26, 58
Morrison, Peter, 25-26
Moose Turd (fly), 108
Muddler Minnow, 73, 74, 75-76, 103
Murry, Tom, 60, 61

New Streamside Guide, 73

No-Hackle, 49
North West Angler, 102
Nymphs, 42
October Caddis, 55, 63-65, 103

Pale Evening Dun, 15
Parachute Adams, 44
parachute fly, 15-17, 49
parachute hackle, 12, 15-17,
Partridge Caddis Emerger, 53
Partridge and Yellow, 51, 52
Peacock, Collie, 23
PMD mayflies, 39, 48, 55
Poly-Wing Spinner, 55, 56
Popular Fly Patterns, 30, 42, 87
Port Townsend Angler fly shop, 39
Puget Sound, 94, 95
Purple Peril, 103, 104, 105

Raccoon (fly), 95, 96, 98-101
Raymond, Steve, 59
Rhyocophila caddisfly, 55
Roaring Fork River, 19
Roche Lake, Canada, 60, 61
Ron's Sculpin, 95, 96
Rosborough, Polly, 42, 43
Royal Coachman, 21, 34
    Hairwing, 21
    Trude, 21-22
Royal Flush, 34-36
Royal Wulff, 21

salmonfly stonefly, 19, 37
Salt Water Fly Patterns, 77
San Juan Worm, 98
Schwiebert, Ernest, 42
scud, 44, 45
    details about, 45

Scud (fly pattern), 44, 45, 46
    fishing, 45
    hooks for, 45
Scud/Freshwater Shrimp (fly), 45
Sculpin, 74, 95
Scheck, Art, 87
Silver Doctor, 85
Silver Outcast, 85-86
Skip Nymph, 99
Skunk (fly), 102
Slough Creek, 25
Smedly, Harold, 21
Smith, Todd, 19
soft-hackled fly, 50-52, 55, 56
    fishing, 50
    hackles for, 50, 51
    tiny, 55, 56
    vs. wet fly, 50, 51
South fork of the Boise River, 19
Sparkle dun, 55, 56, 57

Squash (fly), 98, 99
Starling and Herl, 51, 52
Steelhead Fly Tying Guide, 90
Stewart, Dick, 83, 85, 87
Stewart, Mary, 45
stonefly, 19, 37
    life cycle, 19
Stonefly Angler fly shop, 19
Sunfishes, The, 87
Swisher, Doug, 9

Talleur, Dick, 90, 91
Tapply, "Tap," 83
Tapply, William, 83
Tap's Bug 83-84
termite, 13
thorax dun, 44
tools, fly-tying, for tiny flies, 56
Tom Thumb dry fly, 23-24, 61
Tricorythodes mayfly, 11, 12
Troth, Al, 11, 44, 46
Troth Pheasant Tail, 11
Troth Scud, 44, 46
Trout Fishing, 73
Trude, A. S., 21
Trude dry flies, 21-22
    Lime Coachman Trude, 21-22
    Royal Coachman Trude, 21-22
Tunkwa Lake, Canada, 60
Tunkwanamid, 60-62
Tying and Fishing the Fuzzy Nymphs, 42
"Tying Attractor Flies," video, 9
Tying Flies with Jack Dennis and
    Friends, 25

Versitile Fly Tyer, The, 90
Vissing, Dee, 33

Warmwater Fly Fishing, 83
Waterman, Charles, 85-86
Wayne "Buz" Buszek, 7
Werner Shrimp, 44, 45
Western Angler, The, 59
western March brown mayfly, 55
Wet Bug fly series, 90
wet fly, 49, 50, 51, 52
    vs. soft-hackled fly, 50, 51
Western Trout Fly Tying Manual, 74
Whitlock, Dave, 74
Whitlock Sculpin, 74
Winter's Hope, 102, 103, 104, 106
Wolley, Alan, 25
wet-fly swing, 50
Woolly Bugger, 9

Yakima River, 63

Zebra Midge, 29
Zonker, 79-81